I0517735

MORE THAN BLOODLINES

Releasing Inherited Pain That Was
Never Yours

Copy Editor and Interior Design: Constance Santego
Book Layout: ©2017 BookDesignTemplates.com

Ordering Information:
Quantity sales. Special discounts are available on quantity purchases by corporations, associations, and others. For details, contact the address below.

Trade paperback ISBN: 978-1-990062-77-3

eBook ISBN: 978-1-990062-78-0

Created and published In Canada. Printed and bound in the United States of America

First Edition
Published by Maximillian Enterprises
Kelowna, BC Canada
www.constancesantego.ca

Dedication

To the ones who came before me—
whose whispers live in my bones,
whose pain I carried unknowingly,
and whose strength now helps me release it.
This healing is for all of us.

— Constance

MORE THAN BLOODLINES
Dr. Constance Santego

Maximillian Enterprises
Kelowna, BC

This book is a companion to *AuricIons: Unlocking Subconscious Healing Through Quantum Medicine.* While *AuricIons* introduces the full 9-step method, this volume takes you deeper into Step Seven—exploring the question of *whose* emotion, belief, or burden you're carrying. Together, these books offer a powerful pathway to uncover, understand, and release what was never truly yours.

More Than Bloodlines

Emotional Inheritance, Energy Healing, and the Courage to Let Go

This book is a homecoming. A return to the truths you've always carried. A reawakening of the wisdom stored in your cells, your breath, your story.

It is a bridge — between science and soul, between ancestral weight and spiritual freedom, between the past you inherited and the future you choose.

• It is for the empath who feels too much and wonders why.
• It is for the seeker who senses that their pain isn't all their own.
• It is for the healer who knows that change ripples forward and backward through time.
• It is for the cycle-breaker — the one who says, "It ends with me."

This is not a book about blame. It is a book about release. **A guide to help you identify what was never yours to carry —** and return it, with compassion, back to its source.

Within these pages, you'll explore the emotional threads passed down through generations, learn to listen to your body's hidden wisdom, and journey into the powerful seventh step of the AuricIons Release process — where your soul meets the stories it never chose, and healing begins by naming what no longer belongs.

This is more than personal growth. It is generational alchemy. It is energetic reclamation. It is the quiet revolution of remembrance.

Crafted in healing,
Dr. Constance Santego

ALSO BY DR. CONSTANCE SANTEGO

NOVELS

Illegitimate Grace

Okanagan Trilogy:

Beneath the Vineyards
Under the Okanagan Sun
Guardian of the Lake

The Nine Spiritual Gifts Series:
Journey of a Soul – (Vol 1 Michael)
Language of a Soul – (Vol 2 Gabriel)
Prophecy of a Soul – (Vol 3 Bath Kol)
Healing of a Soul – (Vol 4 Raphael)
Miracles of a Soul – (Vol 5 Hamied)
Knowledge of a Soul – (Vol 6 Raziel)
Wisdom of a Soul – (Vol 7 Uriel)
Faith of a Soul – (Vol 8 Pistis Sophia)

NONFICTION
The Intuitive Life, The Gift Of Prophecy, Third Edition
Fairy Tales, Dreams And Reality... Where Are You On Your Path? Second
Edition
Your Persona... The Mask You Wear
Archangel Michael's Soul Retrieval Guide
Tesla And The Future Of Energy Medicine
Beyond Tesla: *Advancing The Science Of Energy Healing*
Tesla's Code: *Mastering Energy, Frequency, And Creative Power*
BEYOND THE MIND: *HARNESSING THE POWER OF ASTRAL
Projection For Creative Awakening*
Bend, Don't Break: *Finding Your Way Back To Abundance*
Ring Therapy: *A Guide To Healing And Balance*
Ring Therapy Pocket Guide
Floraopathy™: *The Art And Science Of Vibrational Healing With Essential Oils*
Dear Older Me: *A Memoir... Of Sorts*
It's Just Like Poker: *A Spiritual Guide To Playing The
Cards Life Deals You*
Signs And Meanings: *What The Feet Reveal About Health, Stress, And The Body's
Story*
Dear Older Me: A Memoir...*Of Sorts*
Auricions: *Unlocking Subconscious Healing Through Quantum Medicine*The

REIKI WISDOM, SERIES:
Angelic Lifestyle, a Vibrant Lifestyle
Angelic Lifestyle 42-Day Energy Cleanse
Reiki and the Power of The Joint Points: *Unlocking Energy Pathways for Healing*
(Vol I)
Reiki and Karmic Healing: *Releasing Patterns From Past Lives* (Vol II)
Reiki and the Five Elements (Vol III)
Secrets of a Healer, Magic Of Reiki
The Reiki Master's Manual

SECRETS OF A HEALER, SERIES:
Magic Of Aromatherapy (Vol I)
Magic Of Reflexology (Vol II)
Magic Of The Gifts (Vol III)
Magic Of Muscle Testing (Vol IV)
Magic Of Iridology (Vol V)
Magic Of Massage (Vol VI)
Magic Of Hypnotherapy (Vol VII)
Magic Of Reiki (Vol VIII)
Magic Of Advanced Aromatherapy (Vol IX)
Magic Of Esthetics (Vol X)
The Reiki Master's Manual (Vol XI)

ADULT COLORING JOURNALS
SERIES-ZEN COLORING:
Quantum Energy and Mindful Living Journal (Vol 1)
Reiki Energy Journal (Vol 2)
Nine Spiritual Gifts Journal (Vol 3)
I Forgive Journal (Vol 4)

FOR CHILDREN
I am Big Tonight. I Don't Need the Light

COOKBOOK
My Favorite Recipes, with a Hint of Giggle

BUISNESS
How To Use Chatgpt For Authors: *From Idea To Published Book*
Scaling Beyond 6 Figures: *Strategies For Health & Wellness Professionals*
The Academypreneur's Playbook: *Turn Knowledge Into A Revenue-Generating School*

Contents

"We inherit not only our ancestors' genes but their unspoken sorrows."

— *Carl Jung*

Preface

Releasing Generational Patterns That No Longer Serve You

You might've done it already.

Spit in the tube. Mailed it off. Waited for the email that would tell you more about who you are — or where you're from. AncestryDNA. 23andMe. The promise of discovering your roots, your origins, your story.

Maybe you found out you're 12% Irish. 34% West African. 9% Ashkenazi Jewish.
Maybe you discovered a half-sibling you didn't know existed. Or a health marker that raised more questions than answers.

These tests tell you **where** you came from.

But they don't tell you what you carry.

The generational emotional baggage written into your nervous system.

The inherited patterns etched into your energy field.

The beliefs so deeply embedded, they feel like your own thoughts — even when they're not.

They won't explain why your stomach tightens in conflict...

Why you always feel responsible for keeping the peace...

Why you've doubted your worth since before you could put it into words.

DNA doesn't measure emotional inheritance.

It doesn't track the moment your grandfather flinched but said nothing —
the fear etched into his bones, passed down in silence.

It doesn't see the way your mother smiled through shame, teaching you, without words, to hide what hurt.

And it can't explain why you keep repeating a pattern that feels foreign —
like wearing someone else's skin —
because it never belonged to you in the first place.

Yet here you are, carrying it all.
Not by choice. But by blood.
And now, by grace, you get to choose again.

We inherit more than eye color and cholesterol risk.

We inherit beliefs.
Behaviors.
Buried trauma.
Unfinished stories.

And unless we do something about it, we pass them on —
silently, invisibly, unintentionally.

This book is about breaking that cycle.

Taken from the heart of the AuricIons Release process, this practice helps you uncover the hidden roots of what you carry — beliefs inherited, not chosen. Through this work, you'll begin to loosen what was never yours, and reclaim the voice

that always was. You don't have to dig through your whole family tree.
You don't have to know every detail of what happened before you.
You only have to pay attention to what's showing up now.

"The tension in your chest when you try to speak isn't just anxiety — it's generations of silence rising up, asking to be heard."

"The voice that whispers you're too much might not be yours at all — it could be the echo of someone who was once told to shrink, and did."

"The urge to take care of everyone else before yourself may have started as love — but somewhere along your bloodline, it became a survival strategy."

These are the echoes.
Clues from your body.
Signals that something is ready to be seen.

This book won't ask you to relive the past.
It will help you recognize what's been living in you.
And give you a way to finally release it — gently, clearly, fully.

You don't have to carry what didn't begin with you.
And you don't have to pass it on.

You can stop the story here.
And write a new one that's actually yours.

Let's begin.
Dr. Constance Santego

How to Use This Book

This isn't a book you need to race through.
It's a companion — one that walks beside you as you begin to untangle the beliefs you've carried, the pain that never quite felt like yours, and the patterns woven through bloodlines, soul lines, and time.

Some chapters may feel like recognition. Others may stir resistance or unexpected emotion. Both are signs that something meaningful is being touched.

This book explores inherited trauma, ancestral imprints, past-life echoes, and energetic residue — the silent weight that shapes your present even when its origin remains unseen. It also expands on the *AuricIons Release* process — the 9-step method I created a few years ago — to help you trace, witness, and transform what you've unconsciously absorbed or inherited.

If you've already read *AuricIons: Unlocking Subconscious Healing Through Quantum Medicine*, you'll find familiar tools here — but used in a new way.

In this book, we apply the AuricIons method specifically to **Step Seven**: discovering whose energy, emotion, or belief you're actually carrying. Whether ancestral, karmic, or collective, this step asks the question: *"Is this mine?"*

And if you're new to this work? Don't worry. You'll receive the guidance you need to explore these deeper layers at your own pace. You don't need to have read the first book to benefit from the information here — though it may become your next stop if you're called to go further.

You don't have to understand everything at once.
You don't have to believe every concept — just be open to what your body, your inner voice, and your soul might want to show you.

Here's what I suggest:

- **Move at your own pace.** This isn't linear work. Some readers begin at the start. Others skip ahead to the exercises, meditations, or sections that call to them.
- **Pause when needed.** If a memory surfaces or a truth hits deep, stop. Let your nervous system catch up. Breathe. Reflect.
- **Use a journal.** Reflection prompts are woven throughout the book. Writing will help you track patterns, witness shifts, and reclaim your truth in your own words.
- **Explore the Auriclons Release work.** You'll find guided exercises, muscle testing questions, and energetic inquiry tools to help you identify the root of lingering emotional or energetic blocks — whether they began in this life, a past one, or from your ancestral line.
- **Trust your body.** This book encourages you to listen not just with your mind, but with your body — because your body remembers what words may have forgotten.
- **Be gentle with yourself.** This is deep, sacred work. It asks for presence, not perfection. Compassion, not urgency.

This book is a map — not a mandate.
You don't need to rush your healing.
You just need to be willing to follow the threads of sensation, memory, and inner knowing.

Trust your timing.
Honor your process.
And remember — you're not broken.
You're remembering who you were… before the world, your lineage, or your past told you otherwise.

Muscle Testing – A Tool for Inner Clarity

Sometimes the answers we need aren't hidden — they're just quiet.

They don't shout from the mind.
They speak through the body.

That gut feeling you ignored.
The tension that always shows up around certain people.
The way your energy drops when you think of a decision you "should" make.

Your body knows.
And muscle testing is one way to hear what it's been trying to tell you.

In this chapter, we'll go deeper into muscle testing as a tool for accessing inner truth.

You'll learn:

- How to create a neutral starting point (a "yes/no" baseline)
- Techniques you can use solo or with a partner
- The difference between physical response and emotional interference
- Why muscle testing isn't about strength, but alignment

We'll also talk about what can affect your results — hydration, stress, emotional state — and how to approach the process with curiosity, not control.

Muscle testing isn't a magic trick.
It's a practice in presence.
A way to check in with your own inner compass when the outside world is too loud.

And as you begin to tune in, you may be surprised how much your body's been waiting to say.

What It Is, How It Works, and Why It Helps

What is Muscle Testing?

Muscle testing — sometimes called applied kinesiology — is a simple method of asking the body a question and listening for a physical response. It's based on the idea that the body holds information beyond what the conscious mind can access.

By applying gentle pressure to a muscle (often the arm, fingers, or body sway), you can detect subtle changes in strength or resistance. These shifts can reflect internal alignment or stress, offering a yes/no response from the nervous system.

How Does It Work?

At its core, muscle testing measures your body's energetic resonance with a statement, substance, or belief.
When something is true for you — aligned, safe, or beneficial — your body tends to remain strong.
When something is untrue, triggering, or out of alignment — your muscle weakens slightly or your balance shifts.

It's like a built-in lie detector, but instead of detecting deception, it detects **discord**.

This response is part of your autonomic nervous system. The same system that causes your heart to race when you're anxious or makes your stomach clench when something feels "off."

Why Does It Help?
Because your **conscious mind doesn't always know what you believe.**

You might *say* you trust yourself… but your body flinches when someone asks your opinion.
You might *think* you've forgiven a parent… but your energy drops when their name is mentioned.
You might *want* to believe you're worthy… but your muscles weaken when you speak it aloud.

Muscle testing helps you locate the **hidden programming** running under the surface.
It brings what's unconscious into the light — not to judge it, but to **heal it**.

And that's where clarity begins.
Not by thinking harder… but by listening deeper.

Step-by-Step Instructions for Self-Testing (Body Pendulum)

One of the easiest ways to begin muscle testing on your own is through what's called the **body pendulum.**

Your body, when relaxed and grounded, becomes like a pendulum — naturally swaying forward or backward in response to different statements or stimuli. It's a simple yet profound way to bypass overthinking and access your subconscious wisdom.

Before You Begin

- **Stand up straight** in a quiet space, feet shoulder-width apart.
- Make sure you're **hydrated** — water conducts energy.
- Take a few deep breaths to **center yourself.**
- Let your arms rest gently at your sides.
- Soften your knees and unlock your jaw — tension can interfere with results.

Step 1: Establish Your "Yes" and "No"

1. **Say aloud:** "Forward is a yes."
   o Move your body **forward** — this is typically your **yes.**
2. **Then say:** "Backward is a no."
   o Move your body **backward** — your typical **no.**

(If there's no movement yet, take another breath, relax more, and try again. If still not ,go to the bathroom or drink some water.)

Step 2: Ask a Test Question

1. **Say aloud**: "My name is [your real name]."
   - Notice if your body gently **sways forward** — this is typically your **yes**.
2. **Then say**: "My name is [a false name]."
   - You'll likely feel your body **sway backward** — your typical **no**.

Next, form a **clear, present-tense statement** — something your body can respond to energetically.

Examples:

- "I am hydrated."
- "I enjoy my job."
- "It's safe to be seen."
- "This belief is mine."

Speak the statement aloud and wait.

- A **forward sway** indicates **alignment** (yes, truth, resonance).
- A **backward sway** suggests **disharmony** (no, not true, resistance).
- **No movement** means ask a better question.
- **Side to side means** you do not know

Tips for Accuracy

- If your sway is unclear, rephrase the statement more simply.
- Avoid "should" or "need" — stick to statements of fact or belief.
- Keep your energy neutral — don't try to "will" an answer.
- Practice daily to build trust in the process.

Why It Works

Your **body doesn't lie**.
It's constantly scanning your environment — and your inner world — for truth, safety, and alignment.
The body pendulum gives that intelligence a voice.

As you practice, you'll start to notice which beliefs your body supports...
...and which ones it's been trying to let go of all along.

"Did I create this?" vs "Am I holding this for someone else?"

This is the defining question of belief healing.
It's the hinge that turns pain into understanding — and understanding into release.

Ask yourself:

- Is this belief or behavior something I developed in response to my own life or past life?
- Or was it passed down — emotionally, energetically, silently — from someone else's unhealed story?

Most people assume that every thought they think, every fear they feel, and every coping strategy they use must belong to them.
But inherited beliefs don't come labeled.
They just arrive — tucked inside the tone of a parent's voice, the rules of the household, or the atmosphere of silence that surrounded certain topics.

"Did I create this?"

Beliefs you create are typically tied to **direct experiences** — like a childhood wound, a betrayal, or a pattern you developed to protect yourself.

Signs you may have created the belief:

- You remember when or how it started.
- It connects to a repeated experience in your life.
- It feels more recent or logical, even if unhelpful.

Example:

You failed a test in 5th grade and were scolded. Since then, you believe, *"If I'm not perfect, I'll be rejected."*

"Am I holding this for someone else?"

Some beliefs feel **heavier, older**, or strangely out of place. These are often **inherited** — not through genes, but through energetic entrainment and family dynamics.

Signs you're holding it for someone else:

- The emotion feels disproportionate to your actual experience.
- You can't trace it to any specific memory — yet it's deeply familiar.
- It matches your parent's or ancestor's beliefs, behaviors, or wounds.

Example:

You always feel guilty for resting — even though no one has told you you're lazy. But your mother never stopped moving. And her mother worked herself sick. The belief? *"My worth is in my productivity."*

How Muscle Testing Helps

Muscle testing can reveal whether a belief is:

- **Self-created**: originating in your lived experience.
- **Karmic:** Carried over from previous lifetimes, ancestral debts, or soul-level lessons you came into this life to recognize, heal, or complete.
- **Inherited**: absorbed from your family, community, or even cultural lineage.

Each type holds a different frequency—and a different invitation for healing.

Once you identify the origin, healing becomes possible.

You're not betraying your family by releasing what you've inherited.

You're honoring them by choosing freedom.

◆ PART I
Subtle Energy Memory

What You Carry Isn't Always Yours

You were born into more than a family.
You were born into echoes — into stories already in motion.
Some told aloud. Others whispered in silence.

Maybe you've felt it in your bones but couldn't explain it.
A weight you've carried for so long it feels like your own — but
isn't.
The way your body stiffens at conflict, even in peaceful rooms.
How your smile holds back your truth because somewhere, long
ago, someone learned that honesty meant danger.

The constant urge to care for others — to be good, be quiet, be
enough —
even if it costs you your voice.
Even if your nervous system is on fire.

You might have thought it was your trauma.
Your wiring. Your fault.

But what if this pain didn't begin with you?
What if the fear you hold was once your mother's,
and hers before her —
passed down like an heirloom, unspoken but inherited?

This isn't blame.
This is remembering.

Because the moment you realize that what lives in you may have
come *through* you, but not *from* you —
is the moment you become free to release it.

Think about this…Not everything you carry started with you.

Some of it — the anxiety, the guilt, the urge to overachieve or disappear — was shaped by generations past. Passed through nervous systems, spoken in silence, absorbed in early childhood. And while science is beginning to catch up through the study of epigenetics and trauma, we need a deeper lens to truly understand what we've inherited.

Because not all inheritance is biological.
And not all of it makes logical sense.

Let's look at the two core types of imprinting that shape your inner world — even if you never lived the original story:

Genetic Memory

This is the biological imprint — the survival code etched into your DNA.

It includes instinctual responses passed down through generations. Your body may carry echoes of your ancestors' lived experiences, like:

- A heightened startle response, even in safe environments
- Fear or vigilance that seems to have no clear cause
- A deep pull toward self-protection, withdrawal, or distrust
- Reactions that seem too strong for the moment

These patterns are wired into your nervous system and hormonal chemistry — the body's way of saying, *"This once kept someone alive."*

It's not just inherited trauma — it's inherited adaptation.

Energetic Residue

While genetic memory lives in the body, **energetic residue** lives in the field around it.

This is the emotional imprint — the unspoken, unfelt, and unhealed energies absorbed through relationship, environment, and ancestry. It's not encoded in DNA, but in your auric field, your cellular vibration, your emotional blueprint.

You might notice it as:

- Emotions that feel *too big* or *not yours*
- Internal beliefs like "I'm not safe," or "I always mess things up" — even without a known origin
- Resistance to joy, rest, or success — even when you've "done the work"
- Repeating dynamics in relationships that echo your family line

Energetic residue can be absorbed in utero, during early attachment, or passed down energetically through generations. It doesn't belong to your biology — but it can influence every part of your life.

You don't have to untangle where every belief or feeling came from to begin healing.
But understanding the difference between what's embedded in your body…And what's lingering in your energy…
Helps you meet both with clarity and compassion.

Because now, instead of simply asking: **"What's wrong with me?"**
You can ask: **"What am I still carrying — that never started with me?"** And that is where release begins.

The Aura: Where Inheritance Becomes Imprint

What Your Energy Field Knows — Even When You Don't

Long before you had language to name your emotions…
Long before you could make sense of your experiences…
Your energy field — your **aura** — was already recording them.

The aura is not just an abstract concept from spiritual traditions.
It's part of your subtle anatomy — the electromagnetic field that surrounds and weaves through your body, constantly processing input from your inner and outer worlds.

Think of it as your **energetic memory bank.**

But instead of remembering with words, your aura remembers through **vibration**.

It stores:

- Emotional energy you weren't able to express
- Unresolved experiences absorbed from your environment
- Generational imprints passed down without language
- Energetic residue from trauma — even trauma you didn't directly experience

These imprints don't just sit in the background.
They **shape how you respond to life** — even when you don't consciously understand why.

You might feel:

- A rush of panic in response to a harmless tone of voice
- A sense of distrust with someone you've only just met

- An urge to overgive, overfunction, or disappear — on instinct
- A fear of being seen, even when it's safe now

This is your aura reacting to what it recognizes — **even if your mind has no memory of it.**

Why does this matter?
Because the aura carries both your personal history and the echoes of your lineage.
It is the place where emotional inheritance becomes energetic behavior.
It is the link between **epigenetics, entrainment, and energetic residue.**

And importantly — it's also where **healing begins.**

When you work with the aura directly — through intention, awareness, and modalities like energy healing or the AuricIons Release process — you're no longer trying to fix yourself from the surface.

You're meeting the patterns at their source.
You're unfreezing what got stuck.
You're clearing what was never yours to hold.

Because the energy field remembers what the conscious mind forgets.
But it also **responds to choice.**
To presence.
To truth.
To love.

And when you shift the field — you shift the pattern.

Chakras: Where Energy and Emotion Intersect

Most people recognize the **seven chakras** as energy centers aligned with different parts of the body and aspects of well-being — from survival to intuition, identity to spirituality.

But what's often overlooked is that **each chakra also functions as an emotional memory vault.**

These aren't just spinning wheels of energy.
They're intelligent centers that **absorb, process, and store emotional frequencies** — not only from your current life, but potentially from your **ancestral lineage** and even **past-life imprints**.

Each one tells part of your story — and sometimes, the untold stories of those who came before you.

For example:

- **Root Chakra (Base of spine):** May hold the energy of ancestral fear, scarcity, war, or displacement. The fight for survival.
- **Sacral Chakra (Lower belly):** Often absorbs generational shame — especially around emotion, sexuality, or self-expression.
- **Solar Plexus (Stomach area):** Can carry patterns of control, powerlessness, or unprocessed anger passed down through family roles.
- **Heart Chakra (Center of chest):** May hold layers of inherited grief, heartbreak, emotional abandonment, or blocks to receiving love.

- **Throat Chakra (Base of neck):** Tends to store silence — from generations where emotions were suppressed, or voices were dismissed or punished.
- **Third Eye Chakra (Center of forehead):** Can reflect inherited blocks to intuition — shaped by rigid thinking, dogma, or spiritual fear.
- **Crown Chakra (Top of head):** May reveal generational wounds around disconnection from God, worthlessness, or fear of divine punishment.

During **Auriclons Release**, these emotional imprints often surface — not always as memories, but as:

- Sudden tension or pressure in the corresponding body area
- Unexplainable emotions that rise during testing or release
- Images, colors, or phrases tied to the theme of that chakra
- A shift in posture, breath, or voice as energy begins to move

You're not just working with thoughts — you're interacting with an ancient, intelligent system that **remembers on a vibrational level**.

And when distortion is cleared from a chakra, truth and energy flow freely again.

Healing at the chakra level isn't just spiritual.
It's practical.
It realigns how you feel, act, speak, and relate — not just now, but across generations.

Because when you release what was stored in silence, you make space for clarity, connection, and conscious choice.

Let's Recap: How Energy Holds onto the Past—Key Takeaways

Your body holds memory — but so does your energy.
Even after a moment passes, the emotional charge can linger — not only in your nervous system, but in the subtle energetic anatomy that surrounds and animates you.

This is why healing isn't just about mindset.
It's about resonance. And release.

1. Your Aura: A Living Archive

The **aura** is more than a mystical glow — it's a responsive, intelligent field that reflects your inner landscape.
It stores more than just your daily stress. It holds:

- Emotional echoes from your past selves (childhood, adolescence, trauma states)
- Imprints from your family line — especially the unspoken or suppressed
- Vibrational threads from past lives and soul-level experiences

You may not remember the original moment — but your aura does.

This is why certain situations can stir intense reactions with no clear "why." The trigger isn't just in the present — it's echoing something unprocessed from long ago.

2. Chakras: Pattern Keepers

Each **chakra** isn't just an energy wheel — it's a storehouse of frequency and emotion.

It processes, filters, and sometimes **locks in patterns** that were too overwhelming to digest at the time.

These themes often don't begin with you.
They may be echoes of your mother's silence, your grandfather's grief, or generational beliefs about what's "safe" to express.

During **Auriclons Release**, these centers may activate — not always through words, but through sensations, emotions, or intuitive insights.

You're not just observing pain — you're listening to energy that has waited generations to be heard.

Here's how these patterns might show up:

Chakra	Emotional/Inherited Themes
Root	Survival fear, scarcity, instability, abandonment
Sacral	Shame, guilt, emotional repression, sexual trauma
Solar Plexus	Power struggles, control, inherited rage, helplessness
Heart	Grief, loss, guardedness, patterns of over-giving
Throat	Silence, suppression, fear of truth or exposure
Third Eye	Blocked intuition, mistrust, ancestral rigidity
Crown	Disconnection from Source, religious fear, spiritual doubt

3. Energetic Resonance Across Generations

Just like your DNA carries eye color or bone structure, your energy field can carry **vibrational patterns**.
These patterns — abandonment, silence, self-erasure — can ripple through a lineage, unspoken yet deeply felt.

This resonance is absorbed through:

- **Energetic mirroring** in early childhood (watching how emotions are handled or avoided)
- **In utero transmission** of your mother's nervous system and emotions
- **Loyalty to family systems**, where suffering becomes a badge of connection

You may unconsciously repeat behaviors not because they're true for you — but because they were never questioned.

That's not weakness.
That's how energy works: until you bring it into conscious awareness, **it loops**.

4. Why Clearing Is an Act of Love

To clear inherited energy is not to dishonor your ancestors — it's to free them.
To free yourself.
To **choose truth over tradition** when the two no longer align.

Energetic clearing allows you to:

- Distinguish what's yours from what was passed down
- Break patterns of unconscious repetition
- Reclaim your authentic vibration
- Shift the energetic future of your lineage

This is what AuricIons Release is designed to do — not just process what you remember, but help you **release what your energy still carries**.

Because healing doesn't only happen in your mind.
It happens in your **field, your frequency, your felt sense of self**.

And when you clear the inherited weight,
you don't just write a new story for yourself —
you rewrite the energy of your entire bloodline.

Energetic Cords to Family Expectations

You may already be familiar with the idea of energetic cords in relationships — the invisible ties that keep us bound to people, emotions, or memories. But cords don't just connect us to individuals. They also link us to **roles, expectations, and unspoken agreements** within our families.

These cords aren't visible, but they're felt.
As guilt when you choose differently.
As fear when you step out of line.
As pressure to succeed, keep the peace, or never need anything.

They form in childhood, often without words.
You watch your mother sacrifice everything — and feel the pull to do the same.
You sense your father's disappointment — and vow, silently, to never let him down.
You become the caretaker, the achiever, the peacemaker — not because you were asked, but because you were *needed*.
And a part of you still believes that if you stop performing that role, the system might fall apart.

These are energetic cords.

They're not evil or malicious — they were often created out of love, protection, or survival. But they **tether you** to a version of yourself that no longer serves who you are becoming.

Signs You May Be Corded to a Family Role:

- You feel responsible for everyone's emotions
- Saying "no" brings up disproportionate fear or guilt
- You struggle to define your desires outside of what others expect
- You repeatedly abandon your needs to avoid conflict

- You fear that stepping into your truth will "disappoint" someone

The Truth About Cords:

Energetic cords can only stay if the **belief** remains in place.
If you believe your worth is tied to being helpful, you'll stay corded to service.
If you believe love must be earned, you'll stay corded to performance.

The moment you challenge the belief — the cord begins to loosen.

Releasing with Compassion

In the **Auriclons Release** process, when we identify inherited beliefs, we're also locating the cords those beliefs created.

You don't need to sever them in anger.
You can dissolve them in *clarity*.
You can unhook with *honor*.
You can say: "This role helped me survive. But I no longer need it to belong."

This is not rejection.
It's return.
To yourself.

Karma: Pattern, Not Punishment

Not Everything You Carry Comes from This Life

Just as you inherit stories through your DNA and absorb energy through your upbringing, there's another layer — more subtle, more ancient — that may be shaping your present reality:

Karma.

Often misunderstood, karma is not about blame or punishment.
It's not the universe keeping score.
It's not about being "bad" in a past life and "paying for it" now.

Karma, in the context of emotional and energetic healing, is simply this:
Unresolved energy repeating itself — until it's seen, felt, and released.

It's the echo of a soul lesson still unfolding.
It's a pattern circling back for your awareness, not your shame.
Not to make you suffer... but to offer you choice.

Karmic Patterns Often Look Like This:

- A persistent fear of abandonment, even in healthy relationships
- A deep, irrational guilt that doesn't align with your current life
- A tendency to self-sacrifice, dim your light, or silence your voice
- A struggle to feel worthy of love, rest, or abundance — no matter how much inner work you do

These might mirror your upbringing.
They might even look like inherited beliefs from your bloodline.

But sometimes… they didn't start with your family.
They started with **you** — but in another time, another place, another life.

Karma as a Mirror, Not a Sentence

Karmic patterns reflect what's still unhealed within your soul's journey.

They don't come to punish.
They come to **reveal**.

That's why certain people, experiences, or emotions feel *too big, too familiar*, or *too loaded* for the moment.
They're not random.
They're reminders.

Each time a karmic wound resurfaces — in love, in loss, in fear — it's the universe offering you a new way to respond.
To choose differently.
To act from awareness instead of reaction.
To embody wisdom instead of reliving pain.

Reframing Karma Means Reclaiming Power

When you stop seeing karma as something done *to* you…
And start seeing it as something unfolding *for* you…

You begin to:

- Stop blaming yourself for wounds that haven't healed yet
- Recognize yourself as the one who can end the cycle
- Heal on a soul level — not just for you, but for your lineage and lifetimes to come

Karma isn't the jailer.
It's the teacher.
And the moment the lesson is truly integrated — the pattern dissolves.

You're not cursed.
You're conscious now.
And that changes everything.

When the Pattern Isn't Inherited — It's Remembered

Not all emotional imprints come from your bloodline.
Some reach back further — across time, across lifetimes — woven into the memory of your soul.

Just like trauma can pass through DNA, soul-level patterns can pass through incarnations.
They don't live in your family tree.
They live in the energetic threads of your being — showing up again and again until they're acknowledged and transformed.

These karmic patterns can feel nearly identical to ancestral ones.
They land in the same places:

- Your nervous system, as hypervigilance or shutdown
- Your relationships, as recurring dynamics
- Your beliefs, as inner narratives you've never been able to shake

They can feel ancient... and yet intensely personal.

You may find yourself asking:

- *Why does this fear feel so familiar — even though nothing in my childhood explains it?*
- *Why do I attract the same type of partner or betrayal, again and again?*
- *Why do I carry guilt or grief that makes no logical sense?*

This is where soul memory enters the picture.

It's not your imagination.
It's not a flaw.
It's a message from your deeper self.

And it's not here to haunt you —
It's here to free you.

The Path of the Soul Line

Not everything we carry is inherited through blood.
Some threads are older, deeper — woven through lifetimes, not DNA.

A **Soul Line** is a profound spiritual thread that connects you to *all versions of yourself* across time, dimensions, and incarnations. While your bloodline links you to a biological family tree, your Soul Line traces your soul's *evolutionary journey* — through karmic experiences, soul contracts, spiritual gifts, and repeating patterns that transcend generations.

Your soul may have chosen this particular family — not by chance, but by resonance. The wounds you carry may echo not just ancestral pain, but soul-level lessons waiting to be healed.

What Is a Soul Line?

A Soul Line is:

- The unique, evolving path of your soul across time.
- The keeper of karmic imprints, unfinished lessons, and sacred agreements.
- A source of deep spiritual memory that transcends the physical — but may still influence it.
- A mirror that sometimes overlaps with your bloodline — drawing you into families or experiences that reflect unresolved energy from your soul's past.

You might have chosen this incarnation not just to heal your lineage — but to heal yourself across timelines.

Soul Line vs. Bloodline

Aspect	Bloodline	Soul Line
Based on	Genetics / DNA	Consciousness / Spirit
Inherited from	Biological family	Past lives, spiritual realms
Passes down	Physical traits, trauma, beliefs	Karmic lessons, soul gifts, soul-level agreements
Healed through	Therapy, awareness, energy healing	Soul work, regression, forgiveness, spiritual awakening
Felt in the body	Through inherited emotion and survival reflexes	Through intuitive memory, emotional echoes, and spiritual déjà vu

How Do You Know You're Feeling a Soul Line Pattern?

- It doesn't belong to anyone in your known family — but it *feels* familiar.
- You've always carried it — like background noise that followed you here.
- It shows up in dreams, irrational fears, or an intense reaction with no logical origin.
- You've tried to heal it through therapy, yet it lingers — because it wasn't born in this lifetime.

Why It Matters

Acknowledging your Soul Line allows you to go deeper than surface healing.
It opens the door to release not just inherited beliefs — but ancient ones.
To reconnect with not just your family — but your *eternal self.*

Sometimes the root of the pattern is buried so deep, it takes soul-level inquiry to find it.
And that's not about proving anything.
It's about *feeling* what's ready to be released.

From Soul Line to Soul Journey

When you begin to explore whether a pattern is **inherited from family** or **carried forward from a past life**, remember: you are not just unraveling a single thread — you're walking the path of your **Soul Journey**. This journey isn't bound to one lifetime, one family, or even one identity. It's the unfolding of your soul's wisdom through time — a continuous dance of remembering, releasing, and reclaiming. You don't need to know every chapter of that journey to begin healing.

What matters most is feeling into where the residue still lives — in your body, in your beliefs, in your energy. Because the body

remembers what the mind has forgotten. And every moment of presence is a chance to rewrite the story. The most important thing isn't to "prove" where it came from —
It's to feel where it still lives in your body.

Because your body and energy field don't care about timelines.
They care about release.
They care about integration.

The moment you stop trying to trace the pain back to a person —
and instead listen to it as a vibration —
you unlock a new layer of healing.

This is the heart of karmic work:
Not just resolving what was passed to you, but what your soul chose to revisit.

And when you meet that pattern with love and awareness...
You don't just heal this moment.
You rewrite the past.
And you change what's possible in the future.

Ancestral vs. Soul-Level: A Quick Comparison

Question	Ancestral Pattern	Soul-Level Pattern
Origin	Passed through your biological lineage	Carried by your soul across lifetimes
Clues	Similar behaviors, fears, or life experiences as family members	Life themes that repeat even in new environments or unrelated families
Signs	You feel loyal to family pain or stuck in inherited roles	You experience déjà vu, unexplained attraction/aversion, or irrational fears with no known cause
Muscle Test Clue	"Am I holding this for someone in my lineage?"	"Did I experience this in a previous lifetime?"
Intuitive Clue	You sense family emotion or burdens, even if you don't know the story	You feel a sense that the pattern is "older" than this life or family dynamic

When the Lines Blur

Sometimes the roots run in both directions — through your lineage *and* your soul.

You may have chosen this family, this life, precisely because it mirrors something unresolved from your soul's longer journey. This is the essence of **soul contracts** and **karmic repetition**: returning to familiar dynamics, not as punishment, but for the opportunity to transform them.

In these cases, a fear or belief may be **layered** — shaped by ancestral inheritance *and* soul-level memory. If something feels particularly intense, persistent, or resistant to healing, consider that you may be working with more than one origin.

What to Do When It's Both

Whether a pattern is inherited, karmic, or both, healing begins in the same place:

- **Awareness** — Name what you're noticing.
- **Energetic Testing or Intuitive Inquiry** — Use tools like muscle testing or guided introspection to identify the origin.
- **Emotional Release** — Allow the body and energy field to express what's been held.
- **Repatterning** — Consciously choose new beliefs, behaviors, and boundaries aligned with who you are now.

Remember, you don't need to recall the full story of a past life or family trauma to heal its impact.
You only need to recognize what is no longer true for you — and respond with intention.

Because every time you dissolve a layered pattern, you're not just reshaping this chapter of your life...

You're altering the trajectory of your soul — and releasing the hold of history for those who come after you.

Past-Life Beliefs vs. Ancestral Patterns: How to Tell What You're Carrying

Sometimes healing work leaves you with a quiet frustration —
You've explored your childhood.
You've traced family dynamics.
You've journaled, cried, released... and still, something lingers.

It's in that lingering that a deeper question often surfaces:

Is this mine because of my bloodline... or because of my soul's journey?

While ancestral patterns and past-life imprints can feel similar — and often intertwine — they stem from different energetic roots. Distinguishing between them can help you unlock the next layer of healing.

Ancestral Patterns

- Passed down through your **genetic line or emotional inheritance**
- Often echoed in the behaviors, beliefs, or pain of your **parents, grandparents, or even great-grandparents**
- Reinforced by family roles, spoken or unspoken rules, silence, and loyalty

- Triggers often carry a sense of **duty, identity, or belonging** — as if carrying the weight is part of being "one of us"

Common signs:

- "Our family doesn't talk about emotions."
- "We always have to work twice as hard."
- "It's just in our blood to worry."

How it shows up in the body:

- Chronic tension in the shoulders, jaw, chest, or gut
- Subtle hypervigilance or people-pleasing
- Feeling the need to *hold everything together* even when you're falling apart

Past-Life Patterns

- Carried forward **energetically from a previous incarnation**
- Not reflected in your current family — often feels like a personal mystery
- Accompanied by deep, inexplicable **fears, pulls, or aversions**
- Triggers feel **irrational, intense, or untraceable** — as if the emotion belongs to a different lifetime entirely

Common signs:

- Fear of drowning, fire, or abandonment without any related experience
- Persistent guilt, silence, or martyrdom that doesn't match your story
- Repeating patterns in love, loss, or power that seem to follow you across lifetimes

How it shows up in the body:

- Sudden waves of emotion or energetic collapse
- Tightness in the throat or solar plexus with no present-moment cause
- A deep inner knowing — a sense that "this has happened before"

How to Discern the Source

1. Ask clearly and gently — in meditation or muscle testing:
   - *"Am I carrying this for my family?"*
   - *"Did this begin in another life?"*
2. Tune into your inner response:
   - Does it feel like obligation, loyalty, or legacy? → Likely ancestral
   - Does it feel like fate, déjà vu, or karmic entanglement? → Likely past life
3. Look for the mirror:
   - Does your family carry this pattern too? → Ancestral
   - Is it unique to you, persistent, and emotionally disproportionate? → Past life

Why Knowing the Origin Matters

Clarity helps you choose the most effective path forward.

- Ancestral healing may involve lineage work, cord releasing, or family constellation.
- Past-life healing might call for regression, soul retrieval, or energetic clearing.

In the end, *you don't need to remember the story to release the weight.*

You simply need to listen to what your body, energy, and soul are trying to show you — and trust that healing is possible, no matter where the pattern began.

Because the truth is this:

It all led you here.
To remember.
To reclaim.
To release.

Comparison Chart: Inherited Ancestral vs. Karmic vs. Past-Life Patterns

Aspect	Inherited Ancestral	Karmic	Past-Life
Source	Biological lineage — parents, grandparents, ancestors	Soul's energetic memory of choices and consequences	Previous incarnations not linked by bloodline
Transmission Method	DNA, emotional imprinting, modeled behavior	Energetic frequency carried across lifetimes	Soul memory stored in cellular or etheric field
Common Signs	Behaviors or beliefs shared across family members	Repeated lessons/themes across relationships or lifetimes	Unexplainable fears, talents, or dreams

Aspect	Inherited Ancestral	Karmic	Past-Life
Language/Feel	"That runs in the family." "I've always felt responsible."	"Why does this keep happening to me?" "This feels fated."	"I've been here before." "I don't know where this comes from."
Trigger Type	Family dynamics, holidays, inherited roles	Life events that mirror a moral/spiritual imbalance	Certain people, places, or experiences
Healing Methods	Inner child work, family constellation, belief clearing	AuricIons Release, soul contracts, forgiveness, integration	Past-life regression, Akashic healing, energetic release
Goal of Healing	Break family cycles, release inherited burdens	Restore balance, resolve lessons, evolve spiritually	Liberate soul energy stuck in past identities
Muscle Testing Clue	"Did this come through my mother/father's line?"	"Is this my karma from another life or action?"	"Is this from a past-life memory I'm still holding?"
Emotional Tone	Loyalty, grief, obligation	Repetition, frustration, "unfinished business"	Mystery, longing, fear without context

Aspect	Inherited Ancestral	Karmic	Past-Life
Risk if Unexamined	Repeat family pain cycles unconsciously	Delay soul growth through repeating patterns	Stay emotionally tied to identities no longer needed

◆ PART II A New Path to Letting Go

In Case you haven't read it yet... Introducing Auriclons Release

So, what if the feelings you carry—those you can't quite name or trace—aren't actually yours?

What if they belong to a story passed down... a silence absorbed... or a wound inherited from someone else's life?

This is the question that led me to develop *Auriclons Release*—a nine-step method designed to access and clear the deeper energetic imprints that conventional healing often misses. Some of my past students will know it as *Emotional Clearing Technique*.

Not everyone can point to a moment and say, *"That's when it started."*
Sometimes what we carry began long before we had words for it.
And sometimes... it didn't even begin with us.

Years ago, I created *Auriclons Release* from that very mystery.

I designed it for anyone—whether or not they've done the "inner work"—who still feels stuck in something they can't explain.
For those carrying pain, patterns, and beliefs that no longer serve them... or never truly belonged to them in the first place.

And this book, *More Than Bloodlines*, was written to explain on a deeper level exactly that:
For the echoes of sorrow, of survival, of silence that feel far too heavy—and never quite felt like *yours*.

Why This Book Focuses on Step Seven: *Whose Is It?*

In this book, I've dived deeper into **Step Seven**—the moment in the healing journey where you pause and ask:
"Is this truly mine?"

It's a simple question, but it opens profound insight.
You may find that what you've called *yours*—the guilt, the shame, the scarcity, the need to overgive—was never yours to begin with.

This is the step that uncovers:

- Family patterns woven through generations
- Energetic imprints from caregivers or early environments
- Karmic echoes that didn't start in this lifetime

Sometimes it's a parent's fear.
Sometimes a grandparent's silence.
Sometimes, something even older—stored in the **Soul Line**, waiting to be recognized and released.

You don't need to understand the entire history to let it go.
You just need to feel where it lives in your body... and be willing to return it.

In the pages ahead, you'll be guided through the process of recognizing what's truly yours—and what's not. You'll begin the practice of asking the question that changes everything.

Not to blame.
Not to exile the past.
But to finally come home to yourself—clearer, lighter, and more free.

Also, the *Auriclons Release* process uses **muscle testing** to bypass the mind and go straight to the body's wisdom. Because the body doesn't lie. It remembers what the conscious mind forgets—or was never told.

Each of the nine steps is a doorway.
Each one helps you trace and release what no longer belongs in your energetic field.
Some beliefs will come from your own lived experience.
Others… will not.

Unlocking Subconscious Healing Through Quantum Medicine

Dr. Constance Santego
Trade Paperback ISBN: 978-1-990062-49-0
eBook ISBN 978-1-990062-50-6

Why Interruption Matters

Patterns thrive in repetition.
The more often you feel unworthy and shrink back…
The more often you over-give to avoid rejection…
The more often you stay silent to keep the peace…

…the more those pathways get carved into your nervous system.
They become your default.

But defaults aren't destiny.

The moment you do something different — even if it's small —
you send a new signal.
To your body.
To your subconscious.
To your lineage.

Examples of Pattern Interruption:

- Taking a deep breath **before** reacting — instead of rushing to appease.
- Saying, "Let me think about that," instead of your usual automatic "yes."
- Noticing the inner voice of shame — and softly responding, "That's not mine."
- Standing up straight when you want to disappear.
- Choosing rest, even when the guilt creeps in.

These moments may seem small.
But they are revolutions.

Breaking the Spell

When a pattern is interrupted — even once — it loses power.

You stop feeding it.
You stop reinforcing it.
You start choosing instead of reacting.

And over time, that choice becomes your new baseline.

Steps 1-6 of the Auriclons Release in Detail

Unlocking the story behind the symptom—one energetic layer at a time.

Step One: The Problem/Goal — Naming What Needs Attention

Every transformational journey begins with awareness.
In *Auriclons Release*, that awareness starts with **Step One: The Problem**—not because something is "wrong" with you, but because your inner world is asking to be seen, heard, and healed.

Why We Begin Here

Think of Step One as the compass-setting for your healing session.
It answers the simple yet powerful question:

"What are we working on today?"

Sometimes, this answer is clear.
You might come in with something like:

- "I keep attracting toxic relationships."
- "I feel stuck in my career and don't know why."
- "I have anxiety I can't explain."
- "I want to heal a pattern I see repeating in my family."

When that's the case, we **name the issue** and **assign it a number** from **0 to 10**, based on its current intensity.

- *0* means no charge—it feels resolved or neutral.
- *10* means it's highly activated—painful, overwhelming, or present right now.

This number gives you a **baseline**. Not for judgment, but for **tracking your shift**. When you revisit this number at the end of the process (Step Nine), it helps you witness the transformation your energy has undergone—even if your conscious mind can't fully articulate it.

But What If You Don't Know What the Problem Is?

Not everyone begins with clarity.

Sometimes, you just know something's… off.
You feel disconnected.
Emotionally flat or overwhelmed.
Irritable without reason.
Anxious without a clear cause.
Exhausted by life even when "nothing is wrong."

And that's okay.

This step does **not** require a perfect diagnosis or a story that makes sense.

In fact, many of the most profound breakthroughs happen when you **surrender the need to know** and allow the subconscious mind—the true keeper of your inner world—to lead.

Your conscious mind is only the tip of the iceberg.
Your subconscious stores *everything*:

- Memories you've forgotten.
- Emotions you've suppressed.
- Patterns you've inherited.
- Beliefs you never chose.
- Contracts and energy that may go back generations… or lifetimes.

So if your conscious mind draws a blank, you can simply say to your body and subconscious:

"I choose to work on the most important issue or goal for me at this time."

And that's enough.

Your subconscious already knows what's ready to shift.
It knows what's stored in your energy field.
It knows what is **ripe for healing**, even if you don't.

This is the magic of *AuricIons Release*:
You don't have to know the full story.
You just need to be open and willing.

A Note About the Subconscious

The subconscious mind is your **inner archive**, your **emotional processor**, and your **energetic record keeper**.

It logs:

- Emotional experiences (even those you don't remember).
- Beliefs adopted through repetition, trauma, or observation.
- Energetic imprints passed through family or soul lineages.
- Protective mechanisms developed to keep you safe—even if they're no longer needed.

The conscious mind likes certainty, logic, and labels.
But the subconscious speaks in **sensation, symbol, and subtle awareness**.

That's why we use tools like **muscle testing** in AuricIons Release—to bypass the conscious mind and **ask the body directly**.

Reflection Prompts for Step One

If you're not sure what your "problem" is, try asking:

- "What's been bothering me lately—even if I can't explain why?"
- "Where in my life do I feel stuck, small, or overwhelmed?"
- "If I had a magic wand, what would I shift right now?"
- "What's the emotion or pattern that keeps repeating, no matter how much work I've done?"
- "What's the weight I'm tired of carrying?"

Or simply:

"Body, what's ready to be healed?"
"Subconscious, guide me to what's most important right now."

Then pause.
Breathe.
Listen.

Summary: Step One Is an Opening

Whether you're naming a very clear issue or simply showing up with a sense of "something's not right," this step is about **setting the energetic stage**.

It's a conversation starter with your deeper self.

It says: "I'm here. I'm listening. I'm willing."

And that's the most powerful beginning of all.

Practice Prompt:

Think of one situation where you often feel stuck, small, or reactive.
What's the usual pattern?

Now, imagine interrupting it.
What's one different response — even 10% different — that you could try?

Write it down. Practice it in your mind.
When the moment comes, you'll be ready.

And when you interrupt the pattern — you invite healing to begin.

How Your Healing Changes the Collective

You were never meant to carry it all.
But when you choose to heal, you carry something else:
Hope.

Step Two: The Five Bodies

Where is the imprint stored?

You are not just a physical body.
You are a multidimensional being — made of energy, emotion, thought, and soul.

That's why healing must go beyond the surface.
Sometimes a backache isn't just muscular.
Sometimes anxiety doesn't start in the mind.
Sometimes what hurts can't be seen — but can be felt.

In this step, we ask:

Which of the Five Bodies is holding the root of this issue?

The Five Bodies Explained

1. **Physical Body**
   The bones, muscles, tissues, and organs.
   When the issue is here, it may manifest as:
   - o Pain
   - o Illness
   - o Fatigue
   - o Tension or chronic discomfort

2. **Emotional Body**
   The center of feeling, sensitivity, and emotional memory.
   When the issue is here, it might show up as:
   - o Mood swings
   - o Grief
   - o Unprocessed sadness or anger
   - o Emotional reactivity or numbness

3. **Mental Body**
   The realm of thoughts, beliefs, logic, and perception.
   When the issue is here, it may appear as:

- o Negative self-talk
- o Limiting beliefs
- o Overthinking or obsessive thought loops
- o Difficulty focusing or making decisions

4. **Spiritual Body**

The layer of soul connection, purpose, intuition, and divine memory.

When the issue is here, you may feel:
- o Disconnected from meaning or direction
- o Lost, ungrounded, or spiritually blocked
- o As if something larger is trying to get your attention

5. **Energetic / Auric Body**

The subtle field that surrounds and permeates your body. This is where energetic debris, cords, and external influences often live.

When the issue is here, signs might include:
- o Feeling drained or "not yourself"
- o Absorbing others' energy too easily
- o Sensitivity to environments or people
- o A sense that something is "in your field" but hard to name

Why This Step Matters

Knowing **which body is holding the issue** helps you:

- Focus your energy healing more precisely
- Choose the most effective release method in Step Eight
- Understand how the issue is expressing itself (emotionally vs. physically vs. spiritually)
- Honor the **layered nature of healing**

A trauma might be stored emotionally, but show up as chronic pain.
A limiting belief might live in the mental body, but block your spiritual growth.

Or an ancestral pattern might sit in your auric field, quietly influencing everything.

This step helps you get specific.

It says:

"Let's go deeper. Let's find the actual root."

Because when you heal the **right layer**, the shifts ripple outward into all others.

Tip for Practitioners and Self-Use

If you're using muscle testing or a pendulum, simply ask:

"Which of the Five Bodies is holding this issue at the deepest level?"

Allow one to respond clearly before moving forward.
You can always revisit other layers later — but clarity begins with one.

When You Don't Know

Sometimes, the conscious mind can't tell.
That's okay. Let your body guide the answer.

After all, your soul remembers what your mind has forgotten.
And your energy field always knows where to begin.

Step Three: The Chakra System

Which energy center is holding the pattern?

Once we know which body the issue resides in (physical, emotional, mental, spiritual, or auric), the next step is to identify *where* within the energy system the imbalance is anchored.

That's where the chakras come in.

What Are Chakras?

Chakras are spinning energy centers along the spine and body. Each one acts like an energetic storage vault, holding not just your vitality—but also your stories, emotions, memories, and programming. When something unprocessed is held in a chakra, it can create:

- Physical issues in corresponding areas of the body
- Emotional turbulence
- Spiritual disconnection
- Energy blocks that affect your thoughts, relationships, or ability to move forward

Each chakra carries a different theme. Knowing which one is affected brings powerful insight into *what* the issue is about—even before we explore where it came from.

What Each Chakra Represents

1. **Root Chakra (Muladhara)** – *Survival, safety, stability, belonging*
   Blocked when: You feel unsafe, ungrounded, financially anxious, or disconnected from your body or family.
2. **Sacral Chakra (Svadhisthana)** – *Creativity, pleasure, emotions, relationships*

Blocked when: You feel emotionally numb, sexually shut down, stuck in guilt, or creatively blocked.

3. **Solar Plexus Chakra (Manipura)** – *Personal power, confidence, boundaries, identity*
Blocked when: You feel disempowered, indecisive, overly self-critical, or like others control your choices.

4. **Heart Chakra (Anahata)** – *Love, forgiveness, connection, grief*
Blocked when: You struggle with trust, feel emotionally guarded, can't let go of heartbreak, or feel unworthy of love.

5. **Throat Chakra (Vishuddha)** – *Truth, voice, self-expression, boundaries*
Blocked when: You can't speak your truth, feel unheard, or have swallowed too many words to keep the peace.

6. **Third Eye Chakra (Ajna)** – *Intuition, insight, perception, clarity*
Blocked when: You doubt your inner knowing, feel disconnected from your path, or are stuck in confusion.

Crown Chakra (Sahasrara) – *Spiritual connection, purpose, higher self*
Blocked when: You feel spiritually lost, alone in the universe, or cut off from divine guidance.

Why This Step Matters

By identifying which chakra is involved, we begin to understand:

- The *emotional language* of the issue
- What part of your personal development it affects
- Where energy may be stagnant or overactive
- What theme (truth, safety, love, etc.) needs attention to restore flow

This step adds clarity to the vague and unnameable.

It lets your body say:

"Here's where the energy is stuck—and here's what it's about."

Whether the issue is ancestral, karmic, or your own, it leaves an energetic imprint—and the chakras are often the first to register that echo.

How to Use This Step

Using muscle testing or a pendulum, ask:

"Which chakra is most affected by this issue?"
or
"Which chakra is holding this belief or energy pattern?"

You may also receive intuitive insight—a sensation, tightness, or vision. Trust it. Your energy system speaks a subtle but profound language.

Step Four: The Meridian or Organ

What energy pathway or organ is involved—and what does it reveal?

Once we've identified the chakra that's holding the block, we go deeper—into the body's internal energy highways.

This step explores the **meridian system** and corresponding **organs**, giving us a more precise picture of where and how the energetic disturbance is expressing itself.

What Are Meridians?

In Traditional Chinese Medicine (TCM), meridians are invisible pathways that carry **life force energy (Qi or Chi)** through the body. Each one is connected to an organ and associated with a specific emotional and energetic theme.

When energy is blocked or imbalanced in a meridian or organ, it doesn't just create physical symptoms—it also affects your **emotions, thoughts, and behavior patterns**.

Meridian imbalances can be inherited, karmic, or triggered by life experiences.

Examples of Organ/Emotion Associations

Here are just a few of the classic emotional connections from TCM and energy medicine:

- **Liver** – Anger, frustration, feeling stuck
- **Gallbladder** – Indecision, resentment, inner conflict
- **Lungs** – Grief, sadness, inability to let go
- **Large Intestine** – Control issues, holding on to the past

- **Kidneys** – Fear, insecurity, survival panic
- **Bladder** – Anxiety, urgency, emotional overwhelm
- **Heart** – Joy, heartbreak, deep wounding
- **Stomach** – Worry, overwhelm, feeling emotionally "undigested"
- **Spleen** – Overthinking, lack of support, low self-worth
- **Small Intestine** – Discernment, filtering what serves you

Why This Step Matters

Each organ doesn't just serve a biological function—it also acts as an **emotional archive**. Your body remembers what your mind might have long forgotten.

When you identify the meridian or organ holding the imbalance, it:

- Offers insight into the **emotional theme** at play
- Connects symptoms or energetic tension to **root causes**
- Reveals what part of your body is trying to process or protect something unhealed
- Opens a path for targeted release and healing

This is especially helpful when clients say:

"I don't know why I feel this way—I just do."

Often, the body knows.

How to Use This Step

Using muscle testing or a pendulum, ask:

"Which meridian or organ is most involved with this issue?"
Or test directly for individual meridians using a reference chart.

Once identified, reflect on the emotional themes related to that organ. Ask:

- "Does this feeling resonate with the situation?"
- "Where in my life do I feel this kind of energy?"
- "Could this emotion belong to someone else—or another time?"

This is where energy medicine meets body wisdom.

Beyond Biology

You don't need to have physical symptoms to work on an organ energetically. Sometimes, the liver holds anger from generations ago—even if your blood tests look perfect. Sometimes, your lungs ache with grief that isn't yours.

Energy doesn't lie.
And neither does your body.

How Steps 2–4 Help You Understand the Deeper Meaning Behind Step One

When you begin with **Step One,** you're identifying a surface-level problem—something that feels "off," painful, or blocked in your life. But that symptom—whether it's emotional, physical, mental, or spiritual—is just the doorway.

To move from surface to source, you need to ask:
Where is this truly coming from?
Why is this stuck here?
What does it want me to understand, feel, or release?

That's where **Steps 2, 3, and 4** come in.

Step 2: The Five Bodies – Locating the Layer of Disturbance

Your issue might show up as physical pain, emotional overwhelm, mental looping, spiritual disconnection, or energetic exhaustion. By identifying **which body the issue is rooted in,** you:

- Narrow your focus to the **level of reality** that needs attention
- Understand whether the root is **felt** (emotional), **understood** (mental), **embodied** (physical), **energetic,** or **existential** (spiritual)
- Learn where to direct healing—for example, clearing auric imprints vs. soothing nervous system inflammation

Knowing the body affected helps shift the question from "What hurts?" to "What layer of me is carrying the memory of this?"

Step 3: The Chakra System – Revealing the Energetic Theme

Each chakra governs a **core life theme**—like safety, self-worth, truth, boundaries, love, or purpose. When you muscle test which chakra is most impacted:

- You clarify the **life area** the issue is entangled with (e.g., root chakra = survival or security; throat chakra = expression or suppression)
- You identify what may be **unspoken, repressed, or out of alignment**
- You begin to see if this blockage is stopping you from expressing your full self, speaking your truth, receiving love, or trusting life

This gives context to the Step One issue. A vague feeling of anxiety becomes clearer when you realize your **Solar Plexus** is blocked and you've lost your sense of power or control.

Step 4: The Meridian or Organ – Exposing the Emotional Imprint

Now we zoom in further. The **organ or meridian** identified reveals a specific **emotional frequency** being held in the body—whether it's grief in the lungs, anger in the liver, fear in the kidneys, or worry in the stomach.

This step tells you:

- What **emotion** is trapped and needs expression or resolution
- Whether the issue is tied to **suppressed feelings, ancestral imprinting, or unprocessed trauma**
- What part of your body is still carrying the weight of something unresolved

Even when you can't name the original wound, your **organs remember.**

Together, Steps 2–4 Translate the Language of Step One

Let's say your Step One issue is:

"I feel blocked when I try to pursue a new goal. I procrastinate and second-guess myself."

After going through Steps 2–4, you learn:

- Step 2: The blockage is showing in your **mental body** (self-talk and limiting beliefs)
- Step 3: The **solar plexus chakra** is impacted (willpower and self-confidence)
- Step 4: The **liver meridian** is involved (anger and feeling stuck)

Now, you realize this isn't about laziness or poor habits.
It's about old anger—possibly not even yours—living in your body and blocking your confidence.
It's about your mind repeating a belief that you're not allowed to succeed.
It's about an energetic imbalance that's been looping silently beneath your conscious awareness.

Why This Matters

When you *just* name the problem (Step 1), you stay at the level of frustration.

But when you add in:

- **Where it lives** (Step 2),
- **What it's about** (Step 3),
- **What energetic residue it holds** (Step 4)…

You shift from frustration to **insight,** and from insight to the **possibility of transformation**.

This deeper understanding is what allows the next steps in the AuricIons process to work—because you're no longer chasing symptoms. You're tracing the root.

Step Five: The Emotion

Getting to the heart of what your body is holding

Once you've located the general layer of the issue (Step 2), the energetic theme (Step 3), and the organ or meridian involved (Step 4), the next question becomes:

What emotion is this tied to?

Our bodies are emotional archives. Every unprocessed feeling—especially those we weren't allowed or able to express—gets stored somewhere in our system. Over time, these unspoken emotions layer themselves beneath symptoms, behavior patterns, and even personality traits. Step Five helps us uncover that hidden layer.

Why It Matters:

The surface issue might look like procrastination, overgiving, chronic pain, or people-pleasing...
But the core emotion could be **rejection,**

shame, grief, or **abandonment** — emotions that may have been too overwhelming to feel at the time they first arose.

This step is not about digging up pain to relive it. It's about *naming* the emotional thread so you can recognize its influence. Because once an emotion is named, it loses its grip. When it's hidden, it can distort your thoughts, choices, and even how you view yourself — without you realizing why.

What This Step Reveals:

- You might discover that your "anger" is really unacknowledged **betrayal.**

- Or that your chronic tension comes from long-held **fear** of being unsafe.
- Or that your avoidance of success has roots in **guilt** — maybe inherited or culturally absorbed.

It's also possible the emotion you uncover *isn't yours* — it could belong to a parent, ancestor, or even a collective belief passed through your culture or community. Recognizing this opens the door to Step Seven, where you begin tracing *whose* emotion it is.

How We Identify the Emotion:

Muscle testing, intuitive sensing, or guided questioning can reveal the core feeling — even when you don't consciously know it. You may feel it surface in your body as a sensation (tight chest, lump in throat, weight on your shoulders). You might receive a word, memory, or image. Or it may emerge through journaling, breathwork, or simple awareness as you tune in.

The key is to stay open.

Even if the emotion doesn't "make sense" at first, trust that your body knows more than your mind. Your subconscious stores every emotional imprint you've ever encountered — and it knows the exact thread that needs releasing.

In Summary:

Step Five is where your healing becomes deeply personal. You're no longer working with abstract ideas — you're listening to what your body has been trying to say all along. And when you give that emotion a voice, you begin to free yourself from its echo.

Step Six: The Age
When Did It Begin?

Every belief, wound, or energetic imprint has a starting point. Step Six helps us discover *when* that moment occurred — whether in your current lifetime or beyond.

This step isn't just about pinpointing a date on the calendar. It's about tracing the energetic thread back to the origin of the issue. Because when you know **when** something began, you start to understand **why** it took root, **how** it shaped you, and what kind of healing it needs now.

Why This Step Matters

The subconscious mind stores everything — even experiences that happened when you were too young to speak or remember. That time you were left crying in a crib too long? Your nervous system remembers. That moment you felt shame for expressing your needs? It might have planted a seed.

This step allows you to:

- Revisit younger versions of yourself with compassion.
- Understand how early emotional environments shaped current behaviors.
- Recognize that a past life or ancestral event may be influencing your present reality.

Often, clients are surprised to find that a pattern began **long before** the issue became visible. For example:

- A fear of abandonment might trace back to **age 2**, when a parent left for a hospital stay.

- A chronic lack of self-worth might be linked to **age 7**, when a teacher humiliated you in front of the class.
- Or… it may go even further — into **past lives**, where vows, trauma, or soul contracts remain unresolved.

This Life or Beyond?

Using muscle testing, intuitive insight, or guided inner work, you'll first determine:

- Did this originate in **this lifetime** or a **past life?**
- If it's from this life: what **age** were you?
- If past life: is there an image, emotion, or story that emerges?

Even if you don't have a full memory, your body knows. A simple impression — like "around age 4," or "a female figure in another time" — is enough to open the door to transformation.

Why the Timeline Heals

When you connect with the *age* you were when the wound began, something powerful happens:
You activate compassion for that version of yourself (or soul self). You stop blaming your current self for patterns that began in confusion, pain, or misunderstanding. And you allow your system to bring *then* and *now* into alignment — gently dissolving the energetic residue stuck in time.

◆ PART III The Inheritance You Never Chose

Returning What Was Never Yours

You were never meant to carry this.

The guilt that wraps itself around your chest.
The fear that settles in your belly like a quiet tremor.
The belief that love must be earned through perfection or self-sacrifice.

Maybe you've done the inner work.
You've journaled, meditated, gone to therapy—
And yet, something still lingers… like background noise from a story you don't remember choosing.

Because maybe you didn't choose it.

This step is about the moment of deep recognition—when you see with startling clarity that what you've been holding was never yours in the first place.

It may have originated with a mother who lived in constant fear.
A father who believed vulnerability was dangerous.
A great-grandparent who coped by disappearing into silence.

These imprints—these emotional echoes—don't always need to be fixed.
Sometimes, they simply need to be *returned*.

Not rejected.
Not condemned.
But released with love, understanding, and reverence for the survival they once represented.

To honor your lineage is not to carry its pain—
It's to break the cycle with compassion and say,
"This ends with me."

Whether you release through breath, visualization, prayer, or muscle testing, this is your moment to let go.
Not because you're denying the past—
But because you're choosing to shape the future.

Healing doesn't always mean holding on.
Sometimes, it means putting it down.
Gently. Finally. Completely.

Because freedom lives not just in knowing what burdens you carry—
But in the sacred choice to no longer carry them at all.

Step Seven: The Source (Person, Place, Thing or Event)

By now, you've uncovered the layer of your being that holds the issue, the chakra or meridian involved, the emotion that's tied to it, and when it first imprinted. But now comes one of the most revealing steps in the AuricIons process:

THE SOURCE

In this book we are going to focus specifically on... **Who does this really belong to?**

This question opens a powerful doorway.

It may feel like your pain, your fear, your belief — but the deeper truth is often more complex. Many of us carry emotional patterns that were **absorbed, inherited, or imprinted** from others:

- A parent's anxiety you modeled without realizing it.
- An ancestor's survival pattern passed through energy or epigenetics.
- A spiritual echo from a past life or karmic bond.
- A teacher's harsh words or a cultural message you unconsciously accepted.

This step invites you to identify the **original source**. Not to assign blame — but to **bring clarity and compassion** to what was never truly yours to carry.

Using muscle testing or intuitive inquiry, you ask questions like:

- Is this belief or emotion mine?
- Was it inherited?
- Is it from my mother's line? Father's line? Both?

- Is it ancestral, collective, karmic, or past life?
- Is it linked to a specific person, place, or event?
- Do I recognize a pattern that matches someone in my family or history?

This step is not only about "who" — but also about **where and when**. A specific place may hold an emotional residue. A memory may resurface with new meaning. Sometimes you'll see a face, hear a phrase, or feel a presence. That's your body pointing to the origin.

Why does this matter?

Because we cannot fully heal what we misidentify as our own. The moment you realize, *"This didn't start with me,"* you loosen the grip of that energy. You return it — not with blame, but with love.

This step is also a place of **deep empathy**. You may realize your mother lived with fear that was never hers either. You may recognize that an ancestor carried shame they could never speak aloud. You become the one who sees clearly — and **chooses differently**.

When you ask *Whose is it?*, you step into the role of the pattern breaker, the lineage liberator, the conscious soul.

And when the answer arises...
you are no longer the carrier.
You are the witness.
You are the one who lets it go.

The Rise of AncestryDNA and 23andMe

Why We're All Looking for Where We Came From

In the last decade, something remarkable happened.

Millions of people — from all walks of life — spit into a little plastic tube, sealed it up, and mailed it off to a lab.
Not because they were sick.
Not because they were curious about a crime.
But because they wanted to know:
"Who am I, really?"

Companies like **AncestryDNA** and **23andMe** exploded in popularity, turning private questions about heritage into a mainstream ritual.
TV commercials promised connection. Discovery. The thrill of uncovering distant relatives and buried roots.
And people signed up by the millions.

Some were looking for health insights.
Some were searching for family.
But most were just hoping to **understand themselves a little better.**

What they got was data.
Percentages. Geographic clusters.
Maybe even surprise revelations — a sibling you didn't know existed. A grandparent's secret past.
It was fascinating. Sometimes beautiful. Sometimes painful.

But always incomplete.

Because while those tests tell you **where** your people came from...
They can't tell you **what they carried.**

And they can't tell you what they passed down to you — silently, emotionally, energetically.

They don't explain why you tense up when someone raises their voice.
Why you feel the need to prove your worth — even when no one is questioning it.
Why you're always the peacekeeper.
Or why, no matter how far you go, a part of you still feels stuck.

That's the part no test can quantify.

What DNA Testing Can Tell Us — and What It Can't

The Limitations of Science When the Soul Is Involved

DNA testing can tell you a lot.
It can reveal where your ancestors came from.
It can connect you with unknown relatives.
It can identify genetic markers for certain diseases, or trace how your body might respond to specific medications.
It can even tell you whether you're more likely to hate cilantro or need more vitamin D.

It's remarkable.

But it's also… clinical.
Cold, even.
It's data without depth.

Because DNA tests don't tell you:

- Why you freeze up when someone's disappointed in you
- Why conflict makes your heart race

- Why you keep attracting the same kind of emotionally unavailable partner
- Why you've been running your whole life and can't name what from

That's not the kind of thing you can trace through chromosomes.

The Deeper Inheritance

Genetic tests are a beautiful tool — but they focus on traits that can be mapped, measured, or matched.

They don't show what you absorbed in the womb.
They don't explain the emotional aftermath of a miscarriage your grandmother never spoke of.
They don't account for war, migration, addiction, or secrets hidden behind family smiles.

DNA might trace your bloodline — but it doesn't decode your soul-line.

And yet, that's what most of us are truly trying to understand:
Why we feel the way we feel.
Why we live the way we live.
And whether we can finally live differently.

That's where this book comes in.

Because there's a kind of ancestry that isn't written in chromosomes.
It's etched in belief.
In energy.
In the nervous system.
In the inherited patterns we never asked for but live out anyway.

And unlike your DNA...
You can change that.

Navigating Family Dynamics Post-Shift

Healing doesn't happen in a vacuum.
And once you begin releasing inherited beliefs, the people around you may feel it — especially family.

You're not just changing your thoughts.
You're changing the emotional choreography your lineage has danced for generations.
And that shift, even when quiet, can echo loudly.

You Might Find Yourself:

- Saying no where you once said yes.
- Choosing rest over responsibility.
- Speaking up when silence used to feel safer.
- Refusing to play a role you've outgrown.

And that can trigger others — especially if they're still carrying the same patterns you're now releasing.

You're Not Betraying Your Family

You're honoring them by becoming conscious.
You're breaking the cycle, not the bond.

But it may still feel like disconnection — to you or to them.

Some may not understand your changes.
Some may try to pull you back into the old rhythm.

Some may feel abandoned or judged just because you're choosing a different path.

That's normal.

Navigating the Tension

- **Hold compassion and boundaries** at the same time.

  "I love you, and I also need something different now."

- **Don't preach.** People feel safer when you model, not moralize.
- **Let your energy speak.** As you shift, others will feel it — and some will become curious, even if it takes time.
- **Grieve if you need to.** Healing sometimes comes with loss — the loss of roles, identities, and illusions we once held dear.
- **Remember:** You don't need permission to evolve.

For Those Who Feel Alone in the Change

You're not broken for outgrowing the emotional roles you were handed.
You're brave.
You're the one the line's been waiting for.

And the more you live from your truth — peacefully, consistently — the more others will feel what's possible.

Not everyone will follow.
But some will thank you — maybe not with words, but with their own quiet healing.

Boundaries with Compassion

When you start healing inherited beliefs, one of the most radical acts of self-love — and ancestral healing — is setting a boundary.

But boundaries aren't walls.
They're bridges to truth.
They say: "This is where I end and you begin — and I honor both."

Why It's Hard

If your family taught you love means self-sacrifice...
If you were praised for being agreeable, quiet, or the one who held everyone together...
If you learned early that saying no = losing connection...

Then boundaries can feel like betrayal.
Or abandonment.
Or danger.

But the truth is, boundaries **preserve** connection — because they're rooted in clarity, not resentment.

What Compassionate Boundaries Sound Like:

- "I love you. I'm not available for that right now."
- "This isn't about blame. It's about honoring what I need to stay whole."
- "I know this is different. I'm still figuring it out too."
- "I want to stay connected — but in a way that's healthy for both of us."

Compassion Doesn't Mean Self-Abandonment

Being kind doesn't mean staying silent.
Being spiritual doesn't mean being a sponge for others' emotions.
Being loyal doesn't mean living their stories instead of yours.

Try This Practice:

Stand in front of a mirror.
Put your hand on your heart and say:

"I can love you and still say no."
"I can honor you and still choose myself."
"I can be kind without disappearing."

Let your body hear it.
Let your lineage feel it.
This is how the cycle changes — not through force, but through truth spoken with love.

The Map vs. the Territory

Think of your DNA report like a map.
It gives you a broad outline: terrain, origin points, possible paths.
But it doesn't show the terrain of your inner world — the emotional scars, spiritual echoes, or energetic weight passed down through your lineage.

It doesn't tell you how your great-grandmother's loss imprinted on your mother's nervous system, and then on yours.
It doesn't measure the guilt your father carried — or how that shaped the way he parented.
It doesn't show how a family secret, a betrayal, a broken promise left an invisible but very real mark on the generations that followed.

Science is catching up. We now know trauma can be inherited — not just emotionally, but biologically.
Epigenetics has shown that stress, fear, and environmental pressures can influence which genes activate or stay silent — and those changes can be passed on.

But even epigenetics has its limits. It can tell us **that** we inherit emotional patterns. But it can't tell us **how** to heal them.

What Is Epigenetics?

Epigenetics is the study of how your environment and experiences can influence how your genes are expressed — **without changing your actual DNA.**

In other words, the genetic code you inherit doesn't change…
But **how it shows up in your body and behavior can.**

Stress, trauma, malnutrition, emotional neglect, or even a lack of loving connection can leave what's called **epigenetic markers** — tiny chemical tags that tell your genes to turn "on" or "off." These changes can affect how your body responds to fear, bonding, inflammation, and more.

And here's the profound part:
These epigenetic shifts can be **passed down through generations.**

That means a trauma your grandmother lived through — a war, a loss, an unsafe relationship — may still be shaping how your nervous system reacts today.
Your genes didn't mutate.
But your body may have learned to expect threat, or suppress emotion, or stay hyper-alert — because **that's what survival once required.**

Epigenetics offers scientific validation for something many people feel intuitively:
We carry more than just genetic traits.
We carry **survival patterns. Emotional imprints. Generational echoes.**

And the good news?
Just as inherited trauma can be passed down… healing can

ripple forward too.

By becoming aware of what you carry — and choosing new, healthier patterns — you're not only transforming your life... You're changing what gets passed on.

That's the science of **epigenetics** — the study of how life experiences can change the way genes are expressed, without altering the DNA sequence itself.

Think of your DNA as the script.
Epigenetics is the *direction* — what gets highlighted, what gets muted, what gets repeated on loop.

When your great-grandmother lived through famine, her body didn't just survive — it *adapted*. It may have passed on genetic instructions for how to store fat, manage stress, or avoid risk.

When your grandfather returned from war with unspoken trauma, his nervous system remained on high alert. His children — and theirs — may have inherited that vigilance, that fear, that unease.

These changes don't happen through storytelling.
They happen through **cellular memory** — tiny molecular markers that tell your body which genes to turn "on" or "off" based on perceived threats.

Scientific studies now show:

- Children of Holocaust survivors display higher levels of cortisol dysregulation — a marker of chronic stress.
- Descendants of people who experienced severe trauma often carry emotional sensitivity, anxiety, or depression — even if they were never told the full story.
- Trauma doesn't just *impact* a person; it leaves a chemical signature that can be passed on for generations.

But here's the most important part:

Epigenetics is not fate.
What's been passed down can also be turned off.

With awareness, emotional healing, and nervous system regulation, it's possible to **rewrite the signals** your body sends and receives.

This means your healing work today doesn't just help *you* — it shifts the path forward for those who come after you.

You can be the point where the pattern ends.

You can be the interruption — and the new inheritance.

Intergenerational Trauma

The Wounds You Didn't Ask For — But Still Carry

You may be holding pain that never began with you.
And yet it lives inside you — in your body, your breath, your beliefs — as if it were always yours.

That's the quiet power of intergenerational trauma.

It doesn't always announce itself.
There's no headline moment, no obvious origin.
But you feel it.
In the way your shoulders tighten for no reason.
In the panic that rises when someone pulls away — even just a little.
In the exhaustion of trying to stay small so no one gets hurt.

Intergenerational trauma refers to the emotional, psychological, and even physiological wounds that are passed from one generation to the next — often without explanation, language, or conscious intention.

These wounds are not always marked by the event itself — but by the impact that was never processed, never named, and never released.

It can come from:

- A war your grandfather never spoke of
- A mother who buried her grief beneath perfection
- A lineage of silence, survival, or suffering — that shaped the nervous systems of those who came next

You might not know the story.
But you live its echo.

It might show up as:

- **Persistent anxiety** — not from your life, but from inherited hypervigilance passed down as safety.
- **Abandonment fears** — that surface in relationships where nothing has actually gone wrong.
- **Chronic guilt** — for needing rest, for saying no, for simply existing as yourself.
- **Caretaking patterns** — where you've felt responsible for everyone else's emotions since childhood.
- **A drive to prove your worth** — even when you've already earned your place.

These aren't just personal quirks.
They're survival strategies — inherited, embodied, and reenacted across generations.

And while science is still unraveling the full complexity, epigenetics has shown us something crucial:
Unhealed trauma can change the way our genes express themselves.
This means the physiological response to a trauma your ancestor

endured — fear, shutdown, hyper-alertness — can be *biologically* passed on.

But this is not where the story ends. Because you are the turning point.

You have the ability to name what was never named.
To feel what was never safe to feel.
To choose differently — not in blame, but in liberation.

Intergenerational trauma is not a life sentence.
It's an invitation.
To trace the thread.
To rewrite the script.
To say: *It may have started before me… but it ends with me.*

The Body Carries What the Bloodline Couldn't Say

The Patterns You Inherited, The Pain You Never Chose

You were born into more than DNA.
You were born into a rhythm.
A pattern.
A memory your body knows by heart — even if your mind has no words for it.

You may not know your grandmother's sorrow.
Or your father's quiet dread of not measuring up.
You may never have been told about the betrayal, the silence, the fear that threaded its way through generations before you.

But you feel it.

In the tightening of your chest when you try to speak your truth.
In the way your body goes still around conflict — even mild disagreement.
In the pressure to hold it all together, smile, and never ask for too much.

This is inheritance.

Not just in blood or bone, but in behavior.
In belief.
In how your nervous system learned to adapt to an emotional history that predates you.

These hand-me-downs don't always come wrapped in family stories.
They come through gestures.
Through glances.
Through what was modeled, expected, or punished.

You may think:
"That's just how I am."
But pause for a moment — and ask:
What if this isn't me?
What if this is the echo of someone before me who didn't get to heal?

This is **intergenerational trauma.**
The quiet repetition of unspoken wounds.
Passed down not because anyone meant to hurt you —
but because they never had the tools to heal.

It shows up like this:

- Chronic tension that no doctor can explain.
- Emotional reactions that seem "too much" — even to you.
- A lifelong fear of being too loud, too needy, too visible.

- A body that's always braced — even in rest.

These aren't random symptoms.
They're **ancestral signals**.
Your body's way of carrying the truth no one else could say aloud.

Sometimes, your headaches mirror generations of pressure and unspoken duty.
Your gut reflects a family line where intuition was dismissed, danger ignored.
Your clenched jaw is the legacy of words swallowed to keep the peace.

Science now supports what many have always felt:
Emotions are not just experiences — they're imprints.
Stored in the nervous system.
Transmitted through behavior.
Encoded in the body's language of pain, posture, breath, and stillness.

And until you recognize the difference between *what is yours* and *what was passed down*,
you may live someone else's story... thinking it's your own.

But here's the truth:

You are the threshold.
The one who can pause.
Listen.
And choose a new pattern.

This book is an invitation to see your symptoms not as problems — but as maps.
To meet your body not with shame — but with reverence.
Because it has carried more than you know.

And it's ready to let go — not just for you,
but for every ancestor who couldn't.

STORY: "The Toolbox"

When Marco was a boy, his father gave him a box of tools.

Not the kind you buy at the hardware store — though it did hold
a few wrenches and screwdrivers.
This box was different. It came with instructions that were never
written down.

"Be strong."
"Don't cry."
"Handle it yourself."
"Keep going, no matter what."

Marco learned early how to fix things — doors that stuck, sinks
that leaked, feelings that scared his younger sister. He kept his
hands busy and his voice quiet.

By the time he turned forty, Marco could build anything. A
business. A shed. A perfectly logical excuse for why he didn't need
help.
But his body was tired. His heart, heavier than it used to be.

And one day, when his own son fell apart in front of him —
weeping, unraveling over something Marco would've swallowed
whole — Marco felt a strange ache.
Not at his son's pain.
At his own inability to reach for comfort.

He wanted to help.
But all he had was the old box.

So he opened it.

Inside:
Silence.
Sacrifice.
Self-sufficiency, rusted around the edges.
And under it all — fear. That if he put it down, everything would fall apart.

That night, Marco added something new to the box.

A folded piece of paper.

It said:
"It's safe to feel now.
You don't have to build your life out of pain."

And he began the slow work of creating a different inheritance — one that didn't need a toolbox to survive.

Reflection Exercise: What Patterns Run in Your Family Line?

Before healing can happen, awareness must come first.

Not everything that's passed down is painful — but some patterns you've inherited may be quietly holding you back, shaping your choices, or keeping you in a version of life that no longer fits.

This is your moment to pause... and notice.

Ask yourself:

- What roles did the women in your family tend to play? The men?
- Was there space for emotions to be expressed — or were they silenced, minimized, or punished?
- What messages did you absorb about money, love, safety, success, or self-worth?
- Were certain subjects taboo? (Addiction, mental illness, grief, sexuality, ambition?)
- Who was allowed to speak up — and who had to stay quiet?
- Was sacrifice praised more than joy?
- Who felt seen? Who disappeared?

Now go deeper:

- Whose pain have you been carrying, without realizing it?
- Is there a belief in your life right now that feels older than your own experiences?
- When you think about breaking a pattern, do you feel guilt, fear... or freedom?

You may not know all the stories from your family's past.
But your body remembers what your mind has forgotten.
And the patterns you notice — the ones that feel heavy, confusing, or misaligned — are the ones calling for your attention.

You don't have to trace every thread.
Just begin with what feels true.

What are you ready to question?
What are you ready to release?

Because healing your family line doesn't begin with blame — it begins with awareness.
And awareness is what sets the cycle in motion... to end.

How Beliefs Bury Themselves in the Body

We often think of beliefs as thoughts — quiet narratives running through the mind. But the truth is, beliefs are stored far deeper than just the brain. They live in the body.

In your posture.
In your breath.
In the tension you can't quite stretch away.
In the sudden emotional reactions that don't match the moment.

These aren't just mental patterns. They're **embodied imprints** — beliefs that took root through repetition, emotion, and experience. Some began with your own lived moments. Others were inherited, modeled, or absorbed from generations before you. All of them leave an energetic residue that can shape how you move through the world.

Before we can release what's not ours, we must first learn to recognize how it speaks through us — not just in words, but in symptoms, patterns, and sensations.

This book will guide you through the subtle ways beliefs hide in plain sight — in your nervous system, energy field, and cellular memory. You'll begin to notice what you've been carrying… and where it lives in you.

Because healing isn't just about what you *know*.
It's about what your body *remembers*.
And more importantly — what it's ready to let go.

Case Examples: "I Was Born Already Bracing Myself"

Sometimes, we don't need words to know what we've inherited — our bodies already speak the truth.

Here are a few real-life reflections (with identities changed) from people who began to explore the emotional and energetic roots of their inherited patterns:

Case 1: "I was born already bracing myself."
Alex, 38 – Artist

"I've always had this tension in my shoulders. Like I was waiting for the next blow — even when nothing was wrong.
In therapy, we couldn't trace it to anything specific in my childhood. My parents were loving, supportive.
But then I learned that my mother grew up in a house with yelling. Her father had a temper. She never talked about it, but she flinched whenever voices were raised.
I realized… I didn't inherit the trauma directly. I inherited her reaction to it."

Case 2: "I couldn't relax — even when I was safe."
Tasha, 44 – Nurse

"My nervous system was always on. I'd scan rooms. Anticipate problems. I called it being prepared.
But underneath, I was scared — constantly.
Later, I found out my grandmother fled her country during war. She was pregnant with my mom while hiding in a refugee camp.
When I heard that, it made sense. I was born into vigilance. Into survival.
That wasn't mine. But it lived in me."

Case 3: "I didn't know how to receive love."
Markus, 52 – Entrepreneur

"I'd been in therapy for years, but nothing stuck. I kept sabotaging relationships — pushing people away before they could leave me. During a healing session, someone asked, 'Was love safe in your family?'
It hit me. My father lost his younger brother and never recovered. He loved us, but he held back — like if he loved too much, he'd lose us.
I never felt fully chosen, but it wasn't personal. It was protective. Once I saw that, something softened."

These stories aren't about blame.
They're about recognition.

Each person didn't just inherit DNA — they inherited unspoken fear, suppressed grief, and nervous system patterns shaped by past generations.

Case 4: "We're twins — but we carry different ghosts."

Elena and Marie, 31 – Identical twins

"We're twins. Same DNA. Same upbringing.
But somehow, we turned out completely different.

Marie has always been anxious. Always watching the door, scanning for danger.
Me? I'm more avoidant. I shut down when things get hard.

It never made sense… until we looked at our family line.

Our father's mother — our grandmother — lost her first child in childbirth. It was a girl. No one ever talked about her.

Later we found out that our dad was supposed to be 'the replacement baby.' He grew up feeling like he had to be strong, quiet, dependable — so his parents wouldn't break again.

Marie inherited that energy of hypervigilance. Like she had to keep everything under control, or something terrible would happen.

I think I picked up the grief. The silence. I disconnected to survive.

Same womb. Same home.
But we absorbed different emotional blueprints."

What this reveals:
Even with identical genetics and a shared environment, the **energetic inheritance** passed through families can show up differently in each individual — based on personality, birth order, gestational experiences, or even subtle emotional cues from caregivers.

Each sibling, each twin, becomes the "carrier" of a different part of the family's unprocessed history.

But when we begin to name what was unspoken — and release what was never truly ours — healing becomes possible for everyone in the line.

By naming the pattern, honoring its origin, and choosing something new, they began to shift.

And you can, too.

How Your Nervous System Is Shaped Before Birth

The Blueprint You Never Knew You Were Given

Before you ever opened your eyes…
Before you knew what it meant to be "you"…
Your body was already adapting.

Not to your choices — but to someone else's world.
You were cradled inside a body that was reading the environment — moment by moment — and responding with hormones, emotions, and signals that shaped your first experience of life.

In the womb, **your nervous system is not just growing — it's learning.**
Not through thought or language, but through **sensation.**
Through vibration.
Through biochemistry.

When your mother felt joy, your system was bathed in oxytocin — the bonding hormone.
When she felt fear, adrenaline coursed through her body — and into yours.
If she felt overwhelmed, alone, unsupported, or in survival mode, your system registered that, too.

And if her own nervous system had never known rest…
If she inherited anxiety, chronic stress, or emotional shutdown from *her* mother or father…
Then you may have received **a blueprint** that wasn't just hers — but an **emotional legacy** passed down across time.

This isn't about blame.
This is about *biology.*

The Science: What Shapes Your Nervous System

Your **autonomic nervous system** — responsible for regulating stress, safety, and connection — doesn't come fully equipped at birth.
It finishes developing in direct response to your environment:

- Through the tone of voices you hear
- The way you're held or left alone
- The consistency of care — or lack thereof
- The emotional climate in the room

Your developing body takes in every cue and forms a baseline for what "safe" feels like.

This means:

- If your mother was under constant pressure, your body may have normalized vigilance.
- If connection was inconsistent, you may have wired yourself to seek approval — or avoid attachment altogether.
- If love was conditional, your nervous system may have learned to **perform** to be accepted — instead of simply being.

These aren't "bad habits" or "personality quirks."
They are survival strategies formed before you had language — strategies that became **your internal compass.**

Inherited Regulation: The Family Nervous System

Here's what's even more profound:
We don't just inherit trauma through genes.
We inherit **regulation** — or the lack of it.

Your mother's ability to soothe herself was likely shaped by how she was soothed.
Your father's responses to stress were likely modeled by *his* parents.
And so on.

These emotional patterns — the *rhythms of presence, absence, tension, and tenderness* — are handed down like heirlooms, embedded not just in DNA, but in tone, timing, and touch.

We call this **intergenerational nervous system imprinting** — and it can quietly dictate:

- How you respond to intimacy
- How you manage conflict
- Whether your body feels safe in stillness, or only in doing
- Whether your system expects nourishment or neglect

But Here's the Hope:

Neuroplasticity means you can change your story.

Just as your nervous system was shaped by what came before — it can be reshaped by what you choose now.

With support, safety, and **repeated embodied practice**, you can teach your body new cues:

- That rest is safe.
- That love doesn't have to be earned.
- That expression is not dangerous.
- That connection doesn't mean loss of self.

You can **interrupt the cycle.**
Not by rejecting your past — but by gently, powerfully rewriting your response to it.

Every deep breath you allow…
Every time you choose to pause instead of people-please…
Every time you listen to your body's truth instead of overriding
it…
You're not just healing yourself.

You're shifting what becomes possible for those who come after you.

Because just as trauma is passed down…
So is safety.
So is freedom.
So is peace.

Beyond Nature and Nurture: The Power of Energetic Entrainment

What Shapes You Isn't Always What You Can See

For years, the question was framed simply:
Is it nature or nurture?
Are we shaped more by our genetics — or by the environment we grow up in?

Science has made it clear that the answer is **both**.
But there's a third influence — subtle, powerful, and often unspoken — that's just beginning to be understood:
Energetic entrainment.

Let's look at all three:

- **Nature** is the biological blueprint you inherit — the genes passed down from your ancestors, carrying traits, tendencies, and even trauma.
- **Nurture** is the environment that shapes you — the tone of your household, the emotional availability of your caregivers, the lessons you absorbed from how love, anger, or affection were expressed.
- **Energetic entrainment** is what happens beneath words and actions — when your nervous system unconsciously tunes itself to the emotional frequency of those around you.

From the moment you're born — and even before — you're reading the room.
Not with logic, but with **energy**.

Long before you learn language, you understand:

- The tension in someone's jaw
- The tightness behind a smile
- The difference between being looked at and being seen

Your body learns to match what it senses most often.
This is **entrainment** — a kind of emotional mirroring your system does automatically, without thought.
It's not about conscious choice — it's about survival.

And it can look like this:

- If your childhood home was chaotic, your system may become wired for urgency — alert even in moments of calm.
- If emotions were shut down, you may have learned to numb or dismiss your own.
- If love was conditional, you may have internalized the belief that *you* are only worthy when performing, pleasing, or proving.

You didn't need to be told these things.
You **felt** them.
You **matched** them.
You made them your internal "normal."

That's the quiet power of energetic entrainment — it bypasses language and logic.
It's the tuning fork of the soul, vibrating to the frequency of your surroundings.

And it doesn't stop with family.

- Partners entrain to each other.
- Employees entrain to workplace dynamics.
- Communities entrain to collective emotional norms — whether that's resilience or resignation.

You may be carrying **emotional patterns that were never yours to begin with** —
shame that was modeled but never named,
scarcity that was absorbed in glances and gestures,
anxiety that whispered through the walls more loudly than words
ever could.

But here's the good news:
If your system learned to match stress, it can learn to match peace.

Entrainment works both ways.
And your body — resilient, wise, and always listening — is
capable of learning a new rhythm.

By intentionally placing yourself in environments that feel calm,
supportive, and safe...
By choosing relationships where nervous systems co-regulate
rather than compete...
By engaging in practices like breathwork, Reiki, meditation, or
conscious movement...

You begin to **entrain to a different frequency.**

One that doesn't spike your cortisol.
One that doesn't demand your performance.
One that doesn't require you to shrink, hustle, or disappear.

Instead, your body learns to rest.
To trust.
To expand into its full expression.

And this is where the generational shift begins.

Because once you change what your body calls "normal" —
you don't just transform your present.
You rewire the emotional future of your lineage.

Just as trauma can echo through generations, so can healing.

Uncovering What's Not Yours: How Beliefs Get In—and How to Let Them Go

By now, you've likely realized that not every belief you hold started with you. Some entered before you had language—absorbed through energy, emotion, or observation. They whisper in your inner voice, but they're more like echoes: handed down, silently inherited, or unconsciously modeled.

They feel familiar. But that doesn't make them yours.

Signs a Belief Was Inherited—Not Chosen

1. **It feels ancient, not just old.**
   These beliefs don't tie back to a clear moment. They feel like background noise you've always lived with.
   Examples:
   • "I have to earn love."
   • "It's not safe to be seen."
   • "Good things don't last."

2. **It conflicts with your conscious values.**
   You believe in rest, love, or visibility—but shame, fear, or panic still arise when you embrace them.

3. **It operates like an invisible contract.**
   You live by rules you never consciously agreed to:
   • "People like me don't do that."
   • "That kind of life isn't for someone like us."
   • "We don't talk about those things."

4. **It echoes through your family line.**
   Emotional patterns like over-functioning, silence, or scarcity often run generationally. These are not personal flaws—they're inheritances.

5. **It fights back when you try to release it.**
   The strongest clue a belief isn't yours? It brings guilt or fear when challenged. That's not truth—it's loyalty.
   And healing it doesn't dishonor your lineage.
   It honors it—by breaking cycles that were never meant to be permanent.

So where did these beliefs come from?

To clear what's not yours, you must learn to recognize what is.

Truth, Trauma, or Transmission? Learning to Tell the Difference

Just because something feels real in your body doesn't make it true.

Beliefs formed through survival or repetition often feel deeply ingrained. But they're not the same as soul-level truth.

1. Truth is timeless—and liberating.

It feels like breath after suffocation.
It aligns with your essence, not your conditioning.
Examples:
• "I am enough as I am."
• "I deserve rest and love."
• "My voice matters."

2. Trauma is loud—but rooted in survival, not wisdom.

It creates beliefs that feel urgent and absolute—because they once kept you safe.
Examples:
• "I must stay invisible to stay safe."
• "If I don't do it all, it will fall apart."
• "Love always ends in pain."

These are strategies, not identities.

3. Transmission is subtle—but powerful.

These are learned beliefs passed down through emotional modeling or repetition.
They sound like inherited wisdom but feel like emotional contracts.
Examples:
• "Don't be too much."
• "Hope for the best, expect the worst."
• "Put others first, always."

They're often so familiar, they go unquestioned.

How to Discern the Origin of a Belief

Belief Origin	Feels Like...	Leads To...
Truth	Calm, clarity, inner resonance	Freedom, confidence, expansion
Trauma	Fear, tension, urgency	Control, withdrawal, shutdown
Transmission	Familiarity, guilt, self-doubt	Repetition, self-limiting patterns

You don't have to reject your roots to reclaim your truth.

You're allowed to ask:

- "Is this belief expanding me—or keeping me small?"
- "Is this mine—or something I was taught to carry?"

Because the moment you begin remembering what's true for *you*…
You can release what was never meant to stay.

Triggers as Clues: What Your Reactions Reveal

Even when you've identified a belief, the body often holds on.

That's where triggers come in.

Emotional triggers aren't flaws. They're invitations to look deeper. Each strong reaction points to something your body remembers—even if your mind doesn't.

What Is a Trigger, Really?

A trigger is an outsized emotional reaction in a small moment. You might feel an intense surge of emotion when:

- You're interrupted
- Someone dismisses your feelings
- Someone raises their voice
- You witness public vulnerability

Your response might be disproportionate—because it's not just about now. It's echoing a deeper, often inherited imprint.

Signs of Inherited Triggers

You might feel:

• Shame when asking for help
• Panic when receiving praise
• Guilt when resting
• An urge to overwork, over-give, or over-apologize

But your life story doesn't explain these reactions. That's a clue.

Examples:

- A grandmother punished for speaking up.
- A parent who learned love was conditional.
- A great-uncle betrayed for trusting too soon.

These aren't just stories—they're nervous system imprints passed down through behavior, silence, and energy.

What Comes Next?

Now that you've begun thinking about which beliefs may not be yours, you're ready for the next step:

Learning to test and trust your body's wisdom.

In the next section, you'll explore **how to use muscle testing**—a powerful, intuitive tool to verify whether a belief, food, idea, or experience resonates with your energy field or not.

You've questioned the belief.

Now let your body give you the answer.

Extra Muscle Testing Questions

Discovering the Source: Ancestral, Past Life, or Personal?

Here are questions you can ask to determine **whose energy or belief is being held**—specifically to uncover whether it's **ancestral, past life, or someone else's**—using **muscle testing** (or a pendulum, if preferred). These questions are designed to be asked **in yes/no format** for easiest testing:

Muscle Testing Questions for Step 7: WHOSE is it?

Ancestral Lineage (Family/Bloodline)

1. Is this belief inherited from my maternal lineage?
2. Is this belief inherited from my paternal lineage?
3. Did I absorb this belief from my mother?
4. Did I absorb this belief from my father?
5. Is this pattern connected to a grandparent or earlier ancestor?
6. Has this emotional imprint been passed through more than one generation?
7. Is this belief related to a generational trauma or cultural family pattern?

Past Life Origin

8. Is the root of this belief from a past life?
9. Is this energy connected to a karmic contract or lesson?
10. Is this emotional imprint a result of an unresolved experience from another incarnation?
11. Am I carrying a memory or fear from a lifetime where I experienced [insert theme, e.g., betrayal, persecution]?
12. Is this pattern tied to a vow or agreement made in a previous life?

Absorbed from Others (Non-Familial)

13. Did I absorb this emotion or belief from a close friend or romantic partner?
14. Did I take this on from a teacher, coach, or authority figure?
15. Is this belief something I internalized during childhood from someone outside the family?
16. Is this energy connected to a collective trauma or cultural field I was exposed to?

Self-Created or Current Life

17. Is this belief rooted in my current lifetime?
18. Did I create this belief from a personal experience I have had?
19. Is this pattern a defense mechanism developed during a specific time in this life?
20. Is this tied to a childhood event or trauma I experienced directly?

What You've Inherited Isn't What You're Stuck With

You Can Break the Pattern — Without Breaking Yourself

By now, you've seen that what you carry isn't always yours.

You were born into beliefs, behaviors, and emotional climates that shaped you before you ever had the words to name them. And while those patterns may have felt like *truth*, they are not your identity.
They are not your destiny.

They are simply inherited survival strategies — passed down in silence, tension, sacrifice, and gesture.

And survival strategies, once seen, can be transformed.

Healing doesn't mean blaming those who came before you.
It means recognizing what they carried…
What they handed down…
And what **you** now have the chance to release.

Because just as fear is inherited,
so is strength.

The moment you pause to look at the pattern — instead of simply living it — is the moment you become the change agent in your lineage.

You are not here to carry the weight forever.
You are here to remember what freedom feels like — in your body, your breath, your choices.

◆ PART IV The Solution Quantum Medicine Release

With Clarity Comes the Cure

Once you've uncovered the root cause—the age, the emotion, the chakra, and whose energy it is—you're no longer in the dark. The body has spoken. Now comes the most vital part: honoring that truth through release.

In Step Eight, we ask:
"What does the body need to clear this imprint now?"

Using muscle testing or a pendulum, we allow the body's innate intelligence to guide us toward the most aligned method of healing. This isn't a one-size-fits-all process. Your body will choose what works *for you*, in *this moment*.

What Is Quantum Medicine Release?

"Quantum medicine" refers to approaches that address the *energetic root* of an issue—beyond the physical, tapping into the subtle fields where memory, emotion, and vibration intersect. This step is not about logic or prescription. It's about listening to the wisdom of the energy body and meeting the issue at its source.

The methods may include:

- **Hands-on Healing**: Reiki, Therapeutic Touch, or other energy modalities.
- **Vibrational Therapies**: Sound bowls, tuning forks, frequency-specific music.
- **Movement-Based Release**: Dance, stretching, somatic shaking.
- **Mind-Body Practices**: EFT tapping, hypnotherapy, guided visualization.
- **Nature-Based Practices**: Tree grounding, mineral baths, aromatherapy.

- **Creative or Reflective Tools**: Journaling, letter-writing, art therapy, affirmation work.

Why This Step Matters

Many people get stuck at insight. They *understand* the pattern. They *know* it isn't theirs. But they don't know how to move it.

This step transforms knowledge into healing.

Because it doesn't matter how many times you revisit your trauma or talk about your pain—if the energetic imprint stays lodged in your system, the pattern will keep resurfacing.

Release is how we complete the cycle.
Release is how we tell the body:
"We heard you. We're letting it go now."

One Final Note

The subconscious knows what you're ready for.
It will only guide you to methods your body can handle at this time.
So trust it. You don't need to know why that oil, that sound, that movement was chosen—only that your system is asking for it.

Why Letting Go Takes More Than Awareness

As you have read, you didn't just inherit eye color or cheekbones. You inherited stories — sometimes whispered, sometimes shouted, and often never spoken at all.

Stories about who you're allowed to be.
What it means to be "good."
What love should cost.
Who gets to speak, succeed, rest, or belong.

You absorbed those stories — not just through observation, but through energy. Through repetition. Through love.

Because you are not just the product of your past.

You are the author of what comes next.

Why Affirmations Aren't Enough

You've probably tried them.

"I am enough."
"I am safe."
"I deserve love."

You said them in the mirror. Wrote them in journals. Maybe even taped them to your bathroom wall. And yet... something inside didn't shift.

That's because affirmations are like planting seeds on rocky soil.

If the subconscious — the deeper part of you that holds inherited beliefs, old experiences, and energetic imprints — doesn't believe the affirmation, it won't take root.

Affirmations speak to the conscious mind. But most of the patterns driving your behavior, reactions, and self-worth aren't stored there. They live in your nervous system. In your body memory. In the quiet programming inherited through generations.

If a belief like "I'm not safe to be seen" or "I have to earn love" is operating under the surface, no amount of surface-level repetition will override it. The subconscious will reject the new message — not out of sabotage, but out of protection. It's trying to keep you aligned with the "truth" it was taught, even if that truth is painful.

This doesn't mean affirmations are useless.

Mapping Your Emotional Inheritance

You didn't just inherit a family tree — you inherited its roots, its storms, and its seasons of silence.

Some of what you carry isn't in your DNA, but it's still been passed down:
The fear that kept your grandmother quiet.
The anxiety braided into your mother's smile.
The anger your father swallowed until it hardened into distance.

These aren't just personal struggles — they're emotional signatures, woven into the way you respond to life.
And often, we don't even realize we're living someone else's story until we pause long enough to ask:
Where did this really begin?

This chapter is about learning to trace the path backward — not to stay in the past, but to understand how the past is living in you.

Like a map with hidden ink, your emotional inheritance becomes visible when you learn how to look.
We'll explore the tools and questions that help you decode what's been passed down — and begin to separate your truth from your training.

Because healing doesn't mean forgetting where you came from.
It means reclaiming your power to choose where you go from here.

Create Your Personal "Belief Map" or "Inheritance Tree"

Just as you can trace your ancestry through a family tree, you can also trace your emotional lineage — the patterns, beliefs, and coping strategies passed down from those who came before you.

This is your **inheritance tree** — not of bloodlines, but of belief lines.

To create yours, you won't need DNA results or old records. You'll need quiet, reflection, and the willingness to feel into what's been living beneath the surface.

Start by drawing a basic family tree — parents, grandparents, siblings, aunts/uncles, even significant family friends or caretakers. Then ask yourself:

- What was each person's survival strategy?
- What emotions seemed dominant in their life (but maybe never said aloud)?
- What messages did they teach, directly or indirectly, about love, success, safety, or identity?
- What patterns repeated — even across generations?
- What did you witness… and what did you absorb?

As you go, begin to **label patterns** instead of just names:

- "Grandmother – silence = safety"
- "Dad – achievement = love"
- "Mom – anxiety = control"

You're not doing this to blame.
You're doing this to **understand what shaped you — and what you're ready to unshape.**

This process will help you begin to see your life not as a string of isolated struggles, but as part of a larger emotional landscape.
Some of it is yours. Some of it isn't.
Mapping it is how you begin to tell the difference.

Family Memory Timelines

While family trees show who belongs where, **family memory timelines** help reveal *what happened when* — and how it may have shaped the emotional undercurrent running through your lineage.

Events create imprints.
Even if you didn't live through them, their emotional aftermath often echoes into the next generation.

To create a **family memory timeline**, begin by sketching a horizontal line across a page. Then mark off the decades — from your grandparents' childhoods to your own.

Now begin to fill in:

- **Major events**: Wars, immigration, job loss, deaths, divorces, bankruptcies, family feuds, sudden moves, generational secrets.
- **Emotional climate**: Was there a season of silence? A time of high stress? A lingering grief that was never named?
- **Personal stories**: Did someone lose a sibling young? Was love forbidden or survival prioritized over self-expression?
- **Unspoken legacies**: Who didn't talk about their past? Whose name rarely came up? What stories were always told — and which were avoided?

You don't need to know every detail. Intuition matters here. Sometimes what you *suspect* or *sense* is as telling as what's been confirmed.

By laying out the past this way, you may begin to see:

- When patterns started
- Which generation they first appeared in
- How long they've lasted
- And where you're positioned to change them

Because once a pattern is seen, it can be healed.
And when you understand your family's emotional seasons, you can choose to plant something different in your own.

Choosing Your Personalized Path to Letting Go

Now that the hidden belief, block, or pattern has been brought to the surface, it's time for the release.
But not just *any* release — the one that your body, energy field, or subconscious truly responds to.

In this method, we use **muscle testing** or a **pendulum** to identify the most aligned approach — because each person's healing journey is unique.

There are *thousands* of healing tools available. You don't need to know them all. You just need to start with the ones you're drawn to… and be open to discovering more.

Want ideas? In ***AuricIons: Unlocking Subconscious Healing Through Quantum Medicine***, you'll find a curated list of over 30 powerful techniques that support emotional, energetic, and subconscious release — from energy medicine to vibrational tools to creative and spiritual methods.

This book is a companion guide to deeper self-work and is designed to help both practitioners and self-healers choose the method that resonates most.

Available now:

- Trade Paperback ISBN: 978-1-990062-49-0
- eBook ISBN: 978-1-990062-50-6

Let this be your reminder:
You don't have to force healing.
You just have to find the method that speaks your soul's language — and *allow* the energy to shift.

Your Generational Belief Audit

This exercise helps you name what you've inherited — and decide what you're ready to release.

Find a quiet space with a journal, pen, and an open heart. You're not judging or blaming anyone. You're simply observing what's been passed down, and how it may still be shaping you.

Step 1: Identify the Voices

On a piece of paper, write the names of your parents, grandparents, or other key caregivers at the top of separate columns. If someone was absent, that counts too.

Beneath each name, reflect on the following:

- What core beliefs do you associate with this person?
- What emotional patterns did they embody? (e.g., anxiety, martyrdom, control, silence, resilience)
- What phrases did they often say that stuck with you?
- What rules — spoken or unspoken — seemed to define how love, safety, or success were earned?

Don't overthink. Write what comes.

Key Caregivers

Primary Caregivers (Direct Influence)

- Mother
- Father
- Step-parent(s)
- Grandmother
- Grandfather
- Foster parent
- Adoptive parent
- Legal guardian
- Older sibling (in a parental role)

Extended Family (Emotional/Behavioral Modeling)

- Aunt
- Uncle
- Cousins (especially close or older)
- Godparents
- Great-grandparents
- Family elders

Cultural/Community Caregivers (Inherited through societal imprinting)

- Religious leaders (e.g., priest, pastor, rabbi, guru)
- Teachers
- Coaches
- Mentors
- Spiritual guides
- Nannies or babysitters
- Family friends who played parental roles

- Cultural storytellers or elders (especially in Indigenous or ancestral traditions)

Energetic & Karmic Influences (Subtle or soul-level caregivers)

- Soul parents or karmic guardians (spiritual figures from past lives)
- Previous-life family members (whose patterns may continue)
- Collective ancestral energy
- Lineage healers or wounded ancestors (those whose unresolved experiences echo forward)

These caregivers can shape beliefs:

- Through words or silence
- Through actions or absence
- Through love, fear, discipline, modeling, or trauma

Step 2: What Did You Absorb?

Now, turn inward. Consider:

- Which of these beliefs or behaviors do *you* now hold — even if they no longer serve you?
- Which ones feel like yours... and which ones don't?
- Where in your body do you feel them show up? (tight chest, tension in jaw, fatigue, gut reactions)

Mark the patterns that still have a grip on your thoughts, decisions, relationships, or self-worth.

Step 3: Choose What to Keep — and What to Release

For each belief or pattern, ask:

"Does this support who I'm becoming?"
"Was this created by love, or by survival?"
"Is this mine to carry any longer?"

Use a highlighter, symbol, or new column to sort them into:

- **Keep** (wisdom, resilience, healthy values)
- **Release** (outdated fears, limiting roles, survival programming)

This is your **Generational Belief Audit** — your first step in rewriting your inner script.

Because you come from a lineage, yes.
But you're not here to live on repeat.

You're here to heal. To choose. To become the turning point.

Tracing the Echoes of Your Lineage

This isn't just about names on a family tree — it's about the emotional fingerprints they may have left behind.

Whether you've used AncestryDNA, 23andMe, a family Bible, or stories passed down at the kitchen table, this exercise helps you go beyond genetics and explore the context behind your emotional inheritance.

Step 1: Start With What You Know

Draw a simple **three-generation family tree** (you → your parents → your grandparents). Leave space under each name.

Next to each ancestor, write:

- Their **birth and death years** (if known)
- Their **cultural or national background**
- Major life events (war, migration, loss, trauma, success)
- Known **personality traits** or emotional patterns
- Family roles or expectations (e.g., "the fixer," "the silent one," "the provider")

Don't worry if it's incomplete. Even fragments can reveal patterns.

Step 2: Ask Deeper Questions

Now reflect:

- Were any ancestors displaced, orphaned, persecuted, or silenced?
- Did anyone in your lineage lose a parent young? Face poverty or addiction?
- Were there repeating themes — early deaths, strained marriages, emotional absence?
- Which ancestor's story resonates with your own struggles or fears?

These aren't just historical facts — they may be **unprocessed energy** passed through generations.

Step 3: Research What Lives Between the Lines

Use online tools like:

- Ancestry.com
- FamilySearch.org
- Newspapers.com
- Local archives or immigration records

Look for:

- Occupations (Were they caregivers? Soldiers? Servants? Teachers?)
- Causes of death (Patterns of heart issues? Mental health? Accidents?)
- Where they lived — and what was happening historically at that time (wars, economic depression, cultural stigma?)

Let this exploration guide new insight:

"If my great-grandfather lived through a war and never spoke of it… what might he have passed on energetically?"

"If my grandmother raised 9 kids alone, how might that survival-mode be influencing my own relationship to rest or control?"

Step 4: Integrate What You Discover

Take a moment to sit with what you've learned. In your journal, complete these prompts:

- *One story from my lineage that shaped me is…*
- *A pattern I now recognize as inherited is…*
- *Something I now understand — and am ready to release — is…*

You don't need to fix the past.
You just need to stop carrying what no longer belongs to you.

Visual Memory Exercise: What the Photos Don't Say

Photographs are time capsules — not just of appearances, but of unspoken stories, values, and emotional climates.

In this exercise, you'll use old family photos as windows into the lived realities of your ancestors. Beneath the smiles and sepia tones, you may begin to sense the emotional patterns, roles, and beliefs passed down through the generations.

Step 1: Gather the Images

Collect family photographs from your parents, grandparents, aunts and uncles — even digital archives or ancestry profiles. Look for a variety of life stages:

- Childhood photos
- Wedding portraits
- Family gatherings
- Candid everyday moments
- Military or immigration documentation
- Homes, workplaces, vehicles, or possessions

If possible, include both maternal and paternal sides of the family.

Step 2: Observe Beyond the Obvious

Take your time with each photo. Don't rush.

In your journal or workbook, answer these questions for each:

Environment & Context

- Where are they?
- Is the home modest or grand? Urban or rural?
- What objects or surroundings stand out?
- What do their clothes suggest about the era, economic status, or values?

Posture & Expression

- How do they hold themselves?
- Do they look proud, anxious, guarded, joyful?
- Who is placed in the center of the photo? Who is cut off or distanced?
- Are the women or men positioned in traditional or unexpected roles?

Emotional Imprint

- What's the *mood* of the photo?
- If this moment could speak, what might it say?
- Does anything about their expression or body language feel *familiar* to you?

You may begin to see patterns: stoicism, silence, forced smiles, rigid roles, or deep closeness.

Step 3: Zoom Out and Reflect

As you review several photos, ask:

- What kind of life might they have lived?
- What was likely *unspoken* in this family?
- What struggles might have been hidden behind posed smiles or proud suits?
- Do you see patterns repeating — in gender roles, emotional expression, or hierarchy?

For example: "My grandmother was always in the kitchen, smiling — but never beside my grandfather. I've also felt unseen in relationships, over-giving to feel valued."

Step 4: Let the Images Speak

In your journal, try these reflection prompts:

- *When I look at these faces, I feel...*
- *A belief or emotion I see reflected back at me is...*
- *One inherited pattern this photo reveals is...*
- *Something I now want to release is...*

Optional Integration Ritual:
Choose one photo and, with care, write a letter to the person in it — honoring what they endured and gently returning the burden you no longer wish to carry. Thank them for their resilience, and let them know you are choosing a new path.

Energetic Cord Release: The Rooted Clearing Method

This method gently removes cords at the **root** — not just cutting them — so nothing lingers or regrows.

1. Ground and Center

- Find a quiet space.
- Close your eyes and take 3 deep, intentional breaths.
- Visualize roots growing from your feet deep into the earth.
- Feel your energy stabilize and anchor.

2. Identify the Cord

- Bring to mind the person, situation, or belief you feel energetically tied to.
- Notice **where** in your body you feel the connection — chest, gut, back, etc.
- Gently ask: *"What is this cord connected to? What emotion or pattern does it hold?"*

3. Visualize the Cord

- See or sense the energetic cord clearly — its thickness, color, and where it's attached to you.
- Follow it back to its source — person, event, or past version of yourself.

4. Extract the Cord at the Root

- Instead of cutting it (which leaves remnants), imagine your hand (or a divine light) gently **pulling the cord out** — like removing a weed, root and all.

- Breathe steadily as you do this, and **feel the release** as the root detaches completely.
- You might say:

"I release this cord and all its origins, across all time, space, dimensions, and lifetimes.
I keep only the wisdom — and return the rest to Source."

5. Return & Seal the Space

- Visualize healing light — gold, white, violet, or green — filling the space where the cord once was.
- Say:

"I seal this space with love and truth.
I am whole, sovereign, and free."

6. Reclaim Your Energy

- Call your energy back to you:

"I now call all my energy back from this connection — cleansed, cleared, and re-integrated into my highest good."

- Feel it return like waves or light flowing into your field.

7. Thank and Release

- Send gratitude to the situation, person, or belief for the lesson.
- Say: "I release you with love.
We are both free now."

Guided Meditation: "Whose Energy Am I Holding?"

(For Emotional, Ancestral, or Past Life Pattern Awareness)

Begin by finding a quiet space where you won't be disturbed. Sit or lie down in a comfortable position. Close your eyes, and allow your breath to slow.

Breathe in...
Feel the air filling your chest.
Breathe out...
Let the tension fall away.

Inhale again...
Draw your awareness inward.
Exhale...
Softly arrive in this moment.

Let your body settle. Let your thoughts soften. Let your energy begin to speak.

Now gently place one hand over your heart, or wherever you feel a center of emotion in your body.

Bring to mind a *pattern* you've been repeating—a belief, reaction, or emotional trigger that feels heavy, confusing, or persistent. It might be something like...

"I'm never enough."
"I always have to fix everything."
"It's not safe to rest."
"I don't know why I feel this sad."

Just one. Let it rise naturally. No judgment. Just curiosity.

Let this feeling, thought, or memory hover in your awareness.

Now, gently ask yourself:

"Is this truly mine?"
"Did this originate in *my* lived experience—or was it passed to me?"
"Does it feel like it belongs to someone else's story?"

Pause. Breathe. Listen.

Notice what arises—not as a loud answer, but as a *sense*. A feeling. A knowing.

Ask:

"Whose energy might I be carrying?"
"Does this belong to a parent... a caregiver... a sibling?"
"Is it something passed through my ancestral line?"
"Is it something from a past life, a memory beyond time, still seeking resolution?"

You may see a face.
You may feel an emotion not your own.
You may simply sense an old contract whispering from within.

Whatever comes—witness it without fear.

Now, bring your awareness to your body.

Where do you feel this energy?

Your throat?
Your stomach?
Your back or your chest?

Place a hand there, and breathe into that space.

Say softly to yourself:

"I acknowledge this pattern."
"I honor where it came from."
"But I do not need to carry what isn't mine."
"With love and compassion, I choose to release this weight."
"I return it to its source, with peace."

Now imagine a soft light—like a gentle wind or warm water—
flowing through that area of your body.
Washing it.
Clearing it.
Soothing it.

You do not need to know the full story.
You only need to be *willing* to let go of what never belonged to
you.

Feel that light expanding now, softening the edges of your inner
world.

Inhale… And exhale…

When you feel ready, say:

"I reclaim my energy."
"I return to my truth."
"I welcome only what is mine to carry."

Rest here for a few moments longer—feeling lighter, clearer, more
connected to your own essence.

And when you're ready… Begin to return to the room.
Wiggle your fingers and toes.
Open your eyes.

And carry this clarity forward with compassion—for yourself, and
for all those whose stories once became yours.

Guided Meditation: Releasing Ancestral Patterns

Use this meditation after completing Step 7 of the AuricIons Release: Discovering the Origin.

Find a quiet, comfortable place.
Sit or lie down with your spine supported. Close your eyes. Let your hands rest gently on your heart, belly, or anywhere that feels natural.

Take a deep breath in...
And as you exhale, release tension from your body.

Again…
Inhale slowly, deeply…
Exhale fully…
One more time—inhale clarity…
Exhale everything you no longer need in this moment.

Now let your breath settle into its own rhythm.
You are safe here.

Bring to mind the belief, emotion, or sensation that arose in Step 7, whose is this?
The one that didn't feel like it began with you.
Don't analyze it — just notice it. Let it float into your awareness gently, like a leaf on water.

Now imagine this belief as a **thread**, gently extending behind you…
A thread that runs through time.
Through parents, grandparents, great-grandparents…
Maybe even further.

You don't need to see faces or names.
Just feel the **echo** — the way this belief may have woven itself into your family line.
Perhaps it was born from fear… survival… love… loss.
Whatever it was — honor it.

Say silently or aloud:

"I recognize this thread. I thank it for its message.
I no longer need to carry it."

Now place your attention on where you feel this belief or emotion in your body.
Is it in your chest?
Your throat?
Your stomach?
Just notice it — no judgment. You're witnessing.

Breathe into that place.
And as you exhale, imagine light beginning to gather in your body — a soft, healing light.

This light holds **compassion, clarity**, and the power of your conscious choice.

Say to yourself:

"I allow this belief to dissolve.
I release what was never mine to carry.
I choose freedom. I choose truth. I choose peace."

With every breath, the thread loosens.
The energy shifts.
You are not cutting it—you're **unwinding** it… lovingly returning it to Source, to the Earth, or to the ancestors who now cheer you on.

Now ask yourself—gently:

"What is my truth, beyond this inherited story?"

Wait.
Don't rush the answer.
Let your body speak.
Let your soul offer an image… a phrase… a knowing.

Trust what comes.

Take one more deep breath.

Visualize a soft golden light filling the space where that old belief once lived.
Let it wrap around your entire body — like a cocoon of warmth and protection.

Say silently:

"I am whole.
I am free.
I walk forward with clarity and peace."

Begin to return gently.
Wiggle your fingers and toes.
Bring awareness back to the room.
And when you're ready… open your eyes.

*Optional Journal Prompt After the Meditation:

- **What belief or pattern did I release today?**
- **What new truth is ready to take its place?**

Guided Meditation: Releasing the Energetic Weight of Inherited Patterns

Begin by finding stillness.
Sit or lie in a comfortable position.
Allow your breath to slow...
Drop into the space behind your thoughts.
Feel the ground beneath you—supporting, holding, steady.

Inhale gently...
And exhale completely.

Bring to mind a **pattern** you've discovered—one that feels like it didn't begin with you.
Perhaps it showed up in your reactions, your body, your relationships.
Maybe it has no clear origin, just a persistent **energy residue**...
A tension, a fear, or belief that seems woven into your being.

Let it rise gently in your awareness.
You are not judging or analyzing—just noticing.

Say to yourself: "I recognize this inherited pattern.
I see its effect on my life."

Now, imagine this energy connected to a thread —
A long, luminous thread running through **intergenerational time**.
It carries not just stories, but sensations.
It holds **genetic memory**, passed through bodies and breath.
It holds **emotional scars**, passed through silence and survival.
It holds **spiritual echoes**, passed through longing and love.

This thread may carry the **energetic weight** of your ancestors' grief, shame, fear, or sacrifice.

But it also holds their strength.
Their resilience.
Their will to carry on.

Say silently or aloud: "I honor the path before me.
I acknowledge the energy that has shaped me — without letting it define me."

Now scan your body.
Where do you feel this inheritance?
In your **physical body**—a tight chest, aching jaw, heavy limbs?
In your **emotional field**—a sadness that's hard to name?
In your **spiritual self**—a disconnection or doubt?
In your **mental mind**—a thought that keeps repeating?

Just notice.
Witness.
Breathe into it with compassion.

Say: "This memory may live in my body… but it does not need to stay."

Now, with each breath, imagine a soft, healing light entering the place where that memory or energy rests.

This light is **consciousness.**
It is your permission to let go.

As you breathe, the light expands…
Gently lifting the **energetic weight**…
Soothing the **emotional scars**…
Unwinding the **spiritual echoes**…
Transmuting the **genetic memory** into wisdom, not burden.

Say: "This pattern is no longer mine to carry.
I release it with love — for myself and all who came before me."

Feel the thread soften.
Unravel.
Dissolve.

Now ask gently: "What truth wants to take its place?"

Pause.
Let it rise—a phrase, a feeling, a knowing.
Perhaps it's peace.
Perhaps it's joy.
Perhaps it's your power returning.

Let that truth anchor into your physical, emotional, mental, and spiritual layers.
Breathe it in.

Wrap yourself now in a golden cocoon of light.
This light seals in your healing, your sovereignty, your truth.
You are not alone.
You are not broken.
You are becoming whole.

Say: "I am free of inherited weight.
I walk forward as myself—clear, grounded, and renewed."

Wiggle your fingers and toes…
Gently come back to the present.
And when you're ready… open your eyes.

Optional Integration Prompt:

- **What did I feel in my body or heart?**
- **What part of this pattern do I feel ready to release for good?**

◆ PART V Completion – Integration & Closure

Grounding the Healing Into the Present

After all the insight, discovery, and energetic release, Step Nine brings the process full circle. It's where we **pause, reflect,** and **measure.** Not just for results—but for recognition. This is where healing becomes *real* in your body and your awareness.

Reassess the Shift

We return to the original issue or goal and ask:
"On a scale of 0–10, how intense is this now?"

You may find the number has dropped dramatically—or perhaps only slightly. Either way, this check-in reveals movement. Even subtle shifts matter, especially when working at the energetic or subconscious level.

But more importantly, notice what's different:

- Has your body softened?
- Is your breath deeper?
- Do you feel lighter, clearer, or more grounded?

These are the signs that something has begun to move... or even resolve.

Why This Step Matters

Closure is essential. The subconscious mind needs to know when something is complete. This step anchors the work, helping your nervous system recalibrate after energetic change.

Without it, healing can feel disjointed or incomplete—like opening a door but never walking through it.

This step also reinforces self-trust. When you see that the number shifted—or you *feel* something has changed—you learn to trust your body's wisdom, your intuition, and your capacity to heal.

Integration Suggestions

After a session, especially a deep one, take time to:

- **Rest** or take a walk in nature.
- **Hydrate** well—energy work can be detoxifying.
- **Journal** what surfaced, even if it doesn't yet make sense.
- **Create quiet space** to allow the changes to settle.

You've just shifted something that may have been held for years—or even generations. Give your body and soul time to adjust.

Remember

Healing doesn't always end at the session.
Sometimes, shifts continue for days.
Dreams change. Emotions surface. Insights emerge.

Step Nine is not just about closing—it's about *honoring*.
You showed up. You listened. You cleared space for something new.
That deserves acknowledgment.

This is how the cycle completes—
Not with force… but with presence.
Not with perfection… but with peace.
And from here, the next layer—when you're ready—can gently unfold.

Emotional Aftermath of Releasing Inherited Beliefs

Letting go doesn't always feel light at first.

In fact, the emotional aftermath of releasing inherited beliefs can be unexpectedly intense, confusing, or even anticlimactic. You've carried something your whole life—maybe without even realizing it—and now that it's gone, the silence it leaves behind can feel unfamiliar.

You might feel...

- **Lighter** — as though a physical weight has been lifted from your chest or shoulders.
- **Tender** — raw in places you hadn't touched in years, or ever.
- **Emotional** — tears may come without warning, not from sadness, but from deep release.
- **Detached** — like you're watching your life from a new vantage point, no longer entangled in old patterns.
- **Uncertain** — because letting go of a belief means you now get to decide what comes next.

And sometimes, you feel... nothing.
No big epiphany. No dramatic shift. Just a subtle sense that something's different—that you're no longer reacting the same way to the same old triggers.

That's healing.

It's not always loud. It's not always fast.
But it is always real.

In this space of integration, it's important to be gentle with yourself. Rest. Reflect.
Allow your nervous system to adjust to the absence of an old pattern.
Give your body time to rewire around a new truth: *You are no longer bound to what came before you.*

This is the part where healing settles in—not through force, but through trust.

Making Space for Your True Self

When you release what was never yours, you don't just let something go—you make space for something to arrive.

For many, inherited beliefs became the scaffolding of identity. You believed you had to keep the peace... so you never spoke your truth.
You believed love had to be earned... so you overachieved, overgave, over-apologized. You believed you were too much... or not enough... so you dimmed your light or buried your needs.

But those weren't your truths. They were inherited roles. Protective mechanisms. Emotional echoes.

Now that you've set them down, who are you without them?

This isn't a loss—it's a beginning.
In the stillness left behind, your authentic self begins to emerge— not shaped by generational pain, but by present-moment choice.

You may notice:

- A clearer voice when you speak.
- A different posture in your body.
- A deeper calm in situations that used to trigger you.
- A quiet knowing that you are allowed to exist, take up space, and live freely.

This is your invitation to reconnect—with your intuition, your desires, your natural rhythm.
Not the person your lineage trained you to be, but the one you were before the conditioning.

Your true self isn't someone new to become.
It's someone ancient to remember.

Rewriting the Belief System Consciously

Once you've released what doesn't belong, the mind naturally asks: *What now? What do I believe instead?*

This is where the shift becomes intentional.

You're no longer operating on default—living out scripts written generations ago.
You're choosing what stays.
You're choosing what defines you.

Rewriting your belief system isn't about reciting mantras you don't yet believe. It's about gently introducing truths your soul already knows but forgot under the weight of generational noise.

You don't have to force it. You invite it.

This process might look like:

- Asking yourself: *What would I believe if I truly trusted myself?*
- Listening for the quiet truth underneath the inherited fear.
- Feeling into what brings expansion—not contraction—in your body.
- Writing new beliefs that feel like home in your nervous system, not just your mind.

Examples might include:

- *It's safe to speak my truth.*
- *I am not responsible for carrying what others couldn't heal.*
- *I choose to live fully, not small.*
- *Love does not have to be earned.*
- *I can belong without betraying myself.*

This isn't just mental work—it's energetic embodiment.
Each time you act in alignment with your new belief, you reinforce it.
Each time you notice and redirect an old thought, you weaken its grip.

You're not becoming someone new.
You're reclaiming the you that was buried beneath survival.

This is where healing becomes liberation.
Where choice replaces programming.
Where your life starts to reflect who you really are—at last, and on purpose.

Affirmation Repatterning: Rewriting the Energetic Script

Affirmation repatterning isn't about simply saying nice things to yourself and hoping they stick. It's a **deliberate, energetic rewrite** of the beliefs that have shaped your reality—especially those you inherited unconsciously.

Think of it like updating your internal software.

What Is Affirmation Repatterning?

It's the process of replacing an old, inherited belief with a new truth that is:

- Empowering
- Aligned with who you truly are
- Energetically integrated

Unlike generic affirmations, repatterning targets the specific belief you've just released through **Auriclons Release** or intuitive inquiry.

Why Affirmations Often Don't Work

- They're layered **on top** of unhealed pain or false beliefs.
- They're not specific to the pattern or energetic residue you're holding.
- They haven't been tested for **congruence** with your nervous system.
- Your subconscious may reject them if they contradict deeper, unresolved programming.

That's why affirmation repatterning only works **after** you've cleared the space.

The Energy Behind the Words

When you create an affirmation after releasing a false belief, you're not just saying words — you're embedding a **new energetic blueprint**.

It's not about repetition alone.
It's about **resonance**.

Your body and energy system must recognize the truth of the new statement for it to take root.

Example:
Old inherited belief: "I have to stay small to stay safe."
New repatterned affirmation: "It is safe for me to be seen and take up space."

When said after clearing the old pattern, this statement vibrates differently — it becomes **a declaration, not a wish**.

How to Create a Repatterned Affirmation

1. **Identify the Old Pattern**
   "What belief just got released?"
   Example: "I'm a burden."
2. **Ask What's True Now**
   "What do I know to be true instead?"
   Example: "My presence is a gift."
3. **Muscle Test the New Affirmation**
   Ensure your body is congruent with the statement.
   If the body weakens → revise it until it feels truthful and empowering.
4. **Anchor It Energetically**

- o Speak it aloud daily.
- o Write it and place it where you'll see it.
- o Pair it with breath, touch (like hand over heart), or visualization.
- o Use it after meditations, clearings, or as part of your morning ritual.

Affirmation Repatterning in AuricIons Release

This step comes **after releasing** the root belief and testing for neutrality. You're now anchoring your *new truth*.

You might call this:

- "Coding in the new."
- "Truth imprinting."
- "Energetic integration."

Whatever the term, the act is the same: **consciously installing the truth your soul is ready to live.**

"Awareness is powerful — but not always enough. You can journal for years and still feel stuck in the same pattern. That's because some beliefs aren't held in the mind — they're embedded in the body and energy field."

Practice: Creating Your New Truth Script

Now that you've made space by releasing inherited beliefs, it's time to fill that space with intention.

Your *Truth Script* is a personal declaration—a set of beliefs you *consciously choose* to live by. These aren't just affirmations. They're energetic blueprints for the life you're stepping into.

Step 1: Identify the Old Pattern

Start with one belief you've released.
Example: *"I have to stay small to stay safe."*

Step 2: Feel into the Opposite

What would freedom from this belief feel like?
Example: *"I am safe when I express my full self."*

Don't worry about perfection. You're not forcing positivity—you're aligning with possibility.

Step 3: Rewrite with the Body in Mind

Say the new belief aloud.
Does it feel light or tight? Expansive or doubtful?
Adjust until it lands in your body with a sense of *truth*.
Try:

- *"I release the need to hide. My light is safe here."*
- *"I am allowed to take up space, just as I am."*

Step 4: Weave It Into Daily Life

Write 3–5 of these new truths on a card or in your journal.
Speak them each morning—or during moments when old beliefs
show up.
Bonus: Anchor them somatically by placing a hand on your heart,
belly, or solar plexus as you say them.

Step 5: Revisit and Revise

As you heal, your truths may evolve. Let them.
This script isn't fixed—it grows with you.

Example Truth Script

✦ I am worthy without proving.
✦ I carry only what is mine.
✦ I speak with honesty and kindness—and I am heard.
✦ I am rooted in love, not fear.
✦ I am the turning point in my family line.

This isn't about becoming someone new.
It's about becoming *yourself*—the self that was buried under
generations of shoulds and silence.

This is the voice of freedom. And it's yours now.

How the Truth Script Completes the AuricIons Process

The **AuricIons Release** method is designed to walk you through a 9-step process of:

1. Grounding
2. Identifying the issue or belief
3. Muscle Testing to discern its origin
4. Locating it in the body
5. Understanding how it shaped your life
6. Acknowledging who it came from
7. Energetically Releasing the belief
8. Restoring energetic balance
9. Rewriting your truth

Creating your Truth Script is Step 9.

It's the final, integrative step where you no longer just *let go*—you actively *choose what comes next*. Without this step, the release can feel incomplete, like an open space without direction.

Here's why it's vital in the AuricIons system:

- **Energetic Vacuums Need Intention**
  When we release something at the root, we clear emotional, mental, and even physical space. If that space isn't filled with new aligned energy, the old pattern—or another just like it—can sneak back in. The Truth Script *anchors your new frequency.*

- **Muscle Testing Can Confirm Your Script**
  You can use muscle testing to check if the new belief resonates. "Is this the truth I'm ready to embody?" If not, revise until your body says yes. This keeps the new belief

from being just wishful thinking—it becomes an embodied truth.

- **The Soul's Agreement**
  AuricIons isn't about bypassing pain. It's about resolving it at the level of your soul's agreement. When you rewrite your truth, you're declaring a *new agreement with yourself*—one that you chose, not inherited.

- **It Shifts Your Entire Field**
  Thought creates frequency. Belief anchors it. A new script changes the emotional tone you carry—and that ripples out into your decisions, relationships, posture, and presence.

So in essence, your **Truth Script** is the final act of energetic sovereignty in the AuricIons Release process. It's the moment when you stop carrying the echoes of someone else's story and *speak your own into being*.

◆ PART VI Becoming the Cycle Breaker

Who Are You Without the Inherited Weight?

Who Are You Now That You Remember?

Pause.
Breathe.
Feel into the space you've opened—not just in your mind, but in your body, your lineage, your life.

You've traced beliefs back to their roots.
You've named the emotions that once had no words.
You've honored the people they came from—without letting their pain define your path.
You've witnessed how deeply inherited stories can live inside you… and how powerfully they can be released.

So now comes the question:

Who are you now?

Not in the roles you've played.
Not in the wounds you carried.
Not in the masks you wore to stay safe or acceptable.
But beneath it all—in the truth you've reclaimed.

Ask yourself:

• Now that I know how to listen to my body… what will I no longer ignore?
• Now that I've met the younger parts of myself… how will I speak to them with compassion?
• Now that I've seen the patterns clearly… what cycles am I choosing to end?

• Now that I've remembered what's mine—and what's not—what kind of legacy do I want to leave?

This isn't about becoming someone new.
It's about returning to who you were before the world told you otherwise.
Before trauma, silence, or loyalty buried your knowing.
Before you absorbed what was never yours to carry.

You're not broken.
You're not starting over.
You're becoming whole—with your history in your hands, not on your shoulders.

You Are the Turning Point

The healing didn't end with insight.
The real transformation begins in the quiet moments after—
When you pause before reacting.
When you choose presence over pattern.
When you speak a truth that once stayed silent.

This is where the lineage shifts.
Not through grand gestures, but through small, sacred decisions repeated in love.

You won't always get it perfect.
That's not the point.

The point is: **you're aware now.**

You can feel when something old is rising.
You can sense when your body tightens, your breath shortens, your voice quiets...
And you can choose a new response.

This is pattern interruption in its purest form.

It's reaching for kindness when you once reached for control.
It's setting a boundary without guilt.
It's letting yourself rest without proving your worth.
It's forgiving someone—including yourself—not to excuse the past, but to free the future.

You're not here to erase where you came from.
You're here to **alchemize it.**
To gather the wisdom.
To release the pain.
To weave something new from the threads that remain.

You are not the wound.
You are the weaver.
The one who chooses what's passed on—and what is finally put down.

This is your legacy now:
Not survival at all costs.
But truth.
Choice.
Conscious creation.

Let it echo.
Let it anchor.
Let it begin… **with you.**

The Ripple of Your Healing

Your healing doesn't stop with you.
It echoes—softly, steadily—through the branches of your family tree.

Every time you release a belief that's been passed down for generations,
you don't just change your story.
You alter the emotional architecture of those connected to you.

Your children feel the shift.
Your siblings sense it.
Even those who never speak of it notice the difference in your presence—how you move, how you hold space, how you choose.

You become a quiet invitation:
To rest. To feel. To speak. To choose a new way.

Will You Pass Down Pain… or Peace?

Just as trauma can be inherited, so can healing.
When you interrupt a pattern, you plant something new:

• A body that knows how to soften.
• A nervous system no longer braced for threat.
• A lineage rooted not in silence, shame, or fear—but in safety, love, and self-trust.

You become the seed of a new future.

Healing Is a Sacred Contribution

We often think of service as something external—loud, visible, action-oriented.
But tending to your inner world is a radical act of service.

When you heal, the energy around you shifts.
You create space for others to breathe differently.
You show what's possible.
You loosen the grip of old roles.
You name what others couldn't.

Whether they acknowledge it or not—you are the one who opened the door.

Reflect:

Who might feel your healing even if they never name it?
What becomes possible when you hand down peace instead of pain?

Write a letter from a future child, sibling, niece, or nephew—
thanking you for what you chose to break…
and what you bravely chose to begin.

You Are the Legacy

You are not just the product of your past—you are the pivot point.

There is a moment in every lineage when someone rises and says:
"This ends with me."

Not in anger.
Not in blame.
But in reverence—for what was survived, and what now gets to shift.

The silence.
The guilt.
The stories that kept you small—they're not your inheritance anymore.

You get to choose what carries forward.

Legacy Isn't Just What You Build. It's What You Heal.

True legacy isn't found only in family names or accomplishments.
It's in the emotional atmosphere you create.

It's in the courage to tell the truth when silence was expected.
It's in the love you offer freely, without condition.
It's in the joy you let yourself feel—where fear used to live.

It's in your choice to soften, to listen, to stay present when it would've been easier to shut down.

You're leaving more than memories.
You're leaving a new map.

And that… changes everything.

How to Stay Free

Daily Rituals to Hold Your Healing

Healing isn't a one-time event. It's a relationship you build—with your body, your energy, and your truth.

Once you begin releasing generational patterns, the real transformation begins in how you live differently day by day. That's where ritual comes in—not as rigid routines, but as anchors that remind your nervous system: *I'm safe now. I'm free to choose.*

These daily rituals aren't about productivity. They're about presence.
They're the small, sacred acts that help hold the spaciousness you've created through AuricIons Release.

Here are a few soul-nourishing rituals you can begin with:

1. Morning Grounding (5 minutes)
Start your day by reconnecting with your body.
Stand barefoot, place your hands over your heart or belly, and say aloud:

"I am here. I am safe. I am me."

This simple moment reminds your system you don't need to run on survival-mode programming. You're writing new code now.

2. "Is This Mine?" Check-Ins
Throughout the day, when a heavy feeling arises—anxiety, guilt, fear—pause and ask:

"Is this mine... or did I pick it up?"

Even just asking creates space between you and the emotion. Use muscle testing if needed. Or simply breathe and listen to what your body says.

3. Breath for Belief Release

If an old thought pattern resurfaces (e.g., "I'm not enough," "I have to fix everything"), breathe in deeply and imagine exhaling it out of your body.
Then gently say:

"I return this. I choose peace."

The goal isn't to fight the belief—it's to **unhook** from it.

4. Visualize Your Lineage, Healed

Once a week, close your eyes and imagine your family line—parents, grandparents, generations behind you—standing behind you.
See yourself stepping forward with light.
Imagine them smiling, releasing you, saying:

"You're free. Go live."

This simple visualization honors your roots **without keeping you bound to them.**

5. Bedtime Belief Reset

Before sleep, whisper a new truth to yourself.
One that counters the old programming. Something like:

"I am allowed to rest."
"Love doesn't require performance."
"I am safe to be fully me."

Nighttime Is Powerful—Your Subconscious Listens Deeply Here.

The Portal of Night: Where Healing Whispers Loudest

There's something sacred about the hours when the world goes quiet.

When your mind softens, your body unwinds, and the demands of the day finally loosen their grip—your subconscious awakens. This is when the thinking mind steps aside, and the deeper parts of you rise to the surface.

Night is not just for rest. It is a gateway.

Your dreams, your inner voice, even the sensations in your body—these are all channels through which unresolved patterns may reveal themselves. And just as easily, this is when change can slip in undetected, gently rewriting the scripts you've long outgrown.

If you've ever had an epiphany in a dream…
Or woken up feeling lighter after crying yourself to sleep…
Or felt the presence of something greater in the stillness of the dark…

You already know this truth: **Night is when your soul does some of its deepest work.**

So if you choose to do this healing practice before bed—whether muscle testing, journaling, or simply reflecting—know that your subconscious will keep working with it long after you've closed the book.

Before you sleep tonight, try this:

- Whisper your intention out loud, as if tucking it into the folds of your dreams.
- Invite your body to continue releasing what no longer serves you.
- Ask for clarity, comfort, or closure.
- Trust that what rises in the night is your truth, rising to be seen.

You don't need to control the process.
You only need to be open to what the dark reveals—because healing, too, happens in the quiet.

Self-Testing Check-Ins

Once you've learned how to use muscle testing to uncover inherited beliefs, it becomes more than a technique — it becomes a compass. A way to come home to yourself again and again.

Self-testing check-ins are like energetic hygiene. Just as you brush your teeth or wash your hands, this is how you clear what's not yours, tune in to your truth, and stay aligned with the life you're consciously creating.

Here's how to build self-testing check-ins into your day or week:

1. Daily "Truth Touchpoints"

Pick a quiet moment — morning, midday, or night. Take a breath and gently ask:

- "Is my energy mine right now?"
- "Am I carrying anything that isn't serving me?"
- "Did I absorb a belief today that doesn't belong to me?"

Use your preferred self-testing method (like the body sway/pendulum) to get a yes or no. Trust what your body tells you.

If the answer is no — gently say:

"I release what's not mine. I return to my truth."

2. Trigger Response Testing

When you feel suddenly reactive, overwhelmed, or shut down, pause and ask:

- "Is this response familiar from my past?"

- "Am I reacting from my truth… or from inherited fear?"
- "Is there a belief underneath this feeling?"

Muscle testing can help you catch the belief before it takes root again.

3. Weekly Pattern Scan

Once a week, scan your common emotions, thoughts, or body sensations.
Ask:

- "What belief have I been operating from this week?"
- "Is this still true for me?"
- "Did I take on a pattern from someone else?"

If a belief feels heavy, tight, or emotionally charged — it's worth testing.

4. Anchoring the New

When you test for a new truth (e.g., "I am allowed to rest" or "I am worthy of love without earning it"), check how your body responds.

If it tests weak, it means your system doesn't fully believe it yet — and that's okay.

Come back to it. Speak it. Feel it. Let the repetition become reprogramming.

Note: You Don't Have to Obsess

Self-testing isn't about control — it's about curiosity.
If a day feels hard, if an old belief slips through, that's not failure.
That's just another chance to pause, check in, and choose again.

◆ PART VII A Conscious Legacy Is a Sacred Choice

You've traveled far—across timelines, through memory, beneath emotion.
You've uncovered, unraveled, and remembered.
Now, you stand in a different place.
Rooted. Awake.
Aware of the power you hold—not just to heal, but to shape what follows.

Legacy is not only about what you leave behind.
It's about what you refuse to carry forward.

This chapter isn't about crafting perfection.
It's about choosing presence.
It's about letting your life become a living transmission of peace, truth, and permission.

So pause here.
Feel what's different.

Then ask yourself:

- What no longer travels with me?
- What am I planting with my voice, my choices, my energy?
- What atmosphere do I offer the people I love—whether they're here now, or someday will be?

A Living Legacy

You are already becoming someone's ancestor.
Even if you never have children, your energy imprints on the world around you.
In every word, every boundary, every time you soften instead of shut down—you are teaching.

So let your legacy be felt.
Not in what you achieve, but in how you love.

Not in what you control, but in what you set free.
Let it be known: you chose something different.

Practice: The Legacy Letter

Write to your future lineage—biological, chosen, or spiritual.
Let them know what you healed on their behalf.

Tell them:

- What you chose to release.
- What you vowed to protect.
- What you now offer them in return:

Not perfection — but presence.
Not pressure — but possibility.
Not performance — but peace.

Seal it with this truth:

"I did the work, so you could fly freer than I ever knew how."

Let this be your benediction.
Your offering.
Your yes to a different future.

Integration and Forward Momentum

Healing doesn't end with release — it begins there.

You've traced your patterns.
You've met the younger parts of yourself.
You've laid down burdens that were never yours to carry.

You've remembered who you are beneath the noise —
beneath the roles, the loyalties, the survival strategies.

But now comes the quiet art of integration.

This isn't the high of breakthrough or the rush of revelation.
It's the gentle work of living what you've learned —
of weaving your healing into the ordinary.

It's the moment after the ceremony.
The pause after the meditation.
The space where real life resumes —
and you get to meet yourself again, moment by moment.

This chapter is not about doing more.
It's about anchoring what you now know to be true.

Because healing isn't a destination.
It's a relationship.

It's how you:

- Breathe through the next trigger instead of reacting from the wound.
- Notice the familiar pull of an old role—and choose not to perform it.
- Speak gently to the parts of you still learning to feel safe.

- Offer grace to those still trapped in patterns you've begun to leave behind.

Healing becomes embodied when it becomes daily.

It becomes powerful when it becomes practical.

What Integration Looks Like:

- **Returning to your body** as a safe place to land
- **Choosing truth over politeness** when it costs you peace
- **Setting boundaries** as acts of love, not rebellion
- **Creating rituals** that remind your nervous system: I'm safe now
- **Noticing your growth** in the moments you once disappeared
- **Celebrating small shifts** as sacred progress

You don't need to rush.
You don't need to "arrive."
You just need to keep returning.

Returning to your truth.
Returning to your breath.
Returning to your choice.

This is the rhythm now.

You're not becoming someone new.
You're becoming someone free.

And that… is forward momentum.

What Will Your Descendants Inherit From You?

You've done sacred work here.

You've walked through memories that weren't yours and emotions that didn't begin with you.

You've named the invisible.
Broken the unspoken.
Held your lineage in compassion while daring to step beyond it.

This healing wasn't just for your past.
It was a gift to the future.

Because healing doesn't only ripple backward — it echoes forward.
One day, someone will feel the space you created.
The safety you embodied.
The new story you lived into.

So take a moment.
Look ahead.

What do you want them to feel because of you?

Not the weight.
Not the fear.
Not the silence that swallowed generations.

But the freedom to feel.
The courage to rest.
The birthright to choose something different.

Ask Yourself:

- What emotional inheritance am I consciously creating?
- What belief or behavior stops with me?
- What legacy begins — not with achievement, but with awareness?
- What might someone say decades from now because I chose to heal?

Let your answers be tender.
Let them be true.
You don't need to be perfect — only present.

Legacy Letter

To the ones who come after me,

I want you to know…

I chose to look within.
To face what others could not.
To return what wasn't mine — with love, not bitterness.

I chose to soften where others hardened.
To feel where others numbed.
To speak where others stayed silent.

Not so you would be like me —
but so you would be free to be fully yourself.

If you feel more peace, more safety, more permission to exist as
you are…

That is my legacy.

I did the work so you could have wings.
I cleared the path, but the future is yours to shape.

Walk it with courage.
Live it with truth.
And know —
the cycle broke with me…
so it could begin anew with you.

What Do You Believe Now?

As you reach this point in the journey, pause.

You've sifted through generations of stories.
You've returned what wasn't yours.
You've reclaimed the truth of who you are beneath the patterns and pain.

So now ask yourself — gently, honestly:

What do I believe now?

Not what I was taught out of fear.
Not what I inherited in silence.
Not what I carried to make others comfortable.

But what I know — in my bones, in my breath, in my being.

Let this be a moment of reclamation.
Not a list of affirmations you *should* believe —
but a living expression of what feels true today.

Reflection Prompts:

- I believe I am…
- I believe I can…
- I believe I deserve…
- I believe it's safe to…
- I believe it's okay to let go of…
- I believe I was never too much or not enough — just true.
- I believe my healing is…
- I believe my legacy begins with…

These words are not the end of your healing — they're the voice of your integration.

The new script.
The clear signal.

Let them live somewhere visible. Speak them often.
Revisit and revise them as you grow.

Because belief isn't static — it's sacred.
And now that you've cleared the noise, you get to decide what echoes forward.

You are the author now.

Of your beliefs.
Of your story.
Of your future.

Final Auriclons Release Reflection

The Journey Ends, but the Integration Begins

This is not a grand finale.
It's a quiet homecoming.
A return to yourself —
lighter, clearer, more whole than when you began.

You've traveled deep through layers of lineage, emotion, belief,
and identity.
You've asked the brave question:
"Was this ever mine?"
And you've had the courage to listen — and to let go.

Now, as you step into the life you are consciously choosing,
you're invited into one final reflection.
Not to redo the work…
but to witness the shift.

Pause and Ground.

Take a slow breath.
Place your hand on your heart, your belly, or wherever your truth
lives.

Then ask, with compassion:

- What belief have I truly released?
- What truth now feels rooted in my body?
- What part of me feels freer — more authentic — more
  alive?
- What do I now know is mine to carry… and what never
  was?

Write your answers. Speak them aloud.
Or simply let the silence be your witness.

If a new truth or intention is rising, name it.
This is the seed you plant for what comes next —
the frequency you choose to carry forward.

Anchor the Integration.

Close this chapter with this sacred declaration:

**"I return what was never mine.
I keep what is true.
And I walk forward, free."**

You've completed the journey.
But the real work — the conscious living — begins now.

Whenever you feel tangled again…
return to the questions.
When an old story tries to take hold…
return to your breath.
When you forget who you are…
return to this moment.

You don't have to stay *healed*.
You just have to stay *aware*.

Because that —
a life lived awake —
is the legacy you're now leaving behind.

And it began… with you.

◆ APPENDIX

Questions You Might Have

(Or, "Is this woo-woo?" and other things people ask)

"Is this woo-woo or science?"

Both — and neither.

Some of what you'll read in this book is supported by emerging fields like **epigenetics, intergenerational trauma research**, and **somatic psychology**. Other parts — like **muscle testing** or **energy work** — are less measurable but no less impactful for many people.

If it helps: You don't have to believe in energy healing to benefit from it.
You just have to be willing to listen — to your body, your reactions, your own inner truth.

"What if I don't believe in inherited trauma?"

That's okay.

You might not resonate with the term *trauma*. Try thinking in terms of *patterns* or *emotional conditioning*.
Most of us can relate to family dynamics, unspoken expectations, or inherited fears that shaped who we became.

This book isn't about labeling your experience — it's about exploring it.
If something doesn't land, skip it. If it keeps echoing in your thoughts… lean in.

"Can I do this wrong?"

No.

You might muscle test "wrong" at first. You might second-guess an insight. You might forget a step in the AuricIons Release process. That's part of learning — and healing.

What matters is your **intention**.

This work is about coming home to yourself, not performing healing perfectly. Trust that your body, spirit, and subconscious know more than you think. And if you ever feel unsure — pause. Breathe. Ask your body again later.

"Do I have to do all the exercises?"

Not at all.

Think of this book as a buffet. Take what nourishes you. Leave what doesn't (for now). Some tools will feel like immediate relief. Others may not resonate until later.

There is no right timeline — only your own.

"What if I uncover something I'm not ready for?"

Then pause. Breathe. You're in control of this process.

Healing isn't about diving headfirst into pain. It's about gently noticing what's ready to be seen — and honoring your timing. You're allowed to close the book, take a walk, come back later.

You don't have to fix everything at once. You don't even have to fix anything.

Awareness is the first step. Readiness follows in its own time.

"Why do I feel emotional doing this work?"

Because your body is remembering what your mind forgot.

Sometimes, when we explore inherited stories or use tools like muscle testing, unexpected emotions surface. That doesn't mean you're doing it wrong — it means something old is stirring. Something that wants to be felt, so it can be freed.

Tears, tingles, resistance, relief — they're all signs that energy is shifting. Be kind with yourself.

"What if my family doesn't support this?"

You don't need anyone's permission to heal.

This journey is yours — even if those around you don't understand it. And sometimes, when you release inherited patterns, others may feel uncomfortable. That's okay. It doesn't mean you're abandoning them. It means you're choosing a different path — one rooted in awareness, not obligation.

You can love your family and still break their patterns.

"Can I do this work even if I don't know my biological family?"

Yes — deeply, yes.

Even if you were adopted, estranged, or disconnected from your biological lineage, the emotional and energetic patterns you carry are still valid. They may show up through your environment, your early caregivers, or even dreams and intuitive insight.

This book isn't about genealogy. It's about **emotional inheritance** — and your right to release it.

"Will this really change anything?"

If you let it, yes.

You may notice subtle shifts at first: a sense of lightness, a clearer inner voice, a new response in an old situation. Over time, these small changes compound — into new beliefs, new choices, and even new family legacies.

You can't change where you came from.
But you can change what you carry forward.

"What if I don't feel anything when I muscle test?"

That's okay. Not everyone feels a dramatic pull or push.

Muscle testing is subtle, especially at first. It's a skill — and a relationship — between your mind, body, and intuition. Some days will feel more connected than others. The key is to stay curious, not critical. Even simply asking the question begins to shift energy.

And if it never clicks for you? That's fine too. There are other ways to access your truth.

"Do I need to believe in energy to benefit from this book?"

No — but it helps to believe in **yourself.**

Energy is just information in motion. Whether you call it "intuition," "gut feeling," "resonance," or "vibe," most of us have felt it. You don't need to believe in anything mystical. You just need to believe that your body remembers, and that your story matters.

This book is less about belief, and more about awareness. That's where healing begins.

"What if I find myself resisting this work?"

Then something is waking up.

Resistance isn't failure — it's a form of self-protection. Sometimes our inner systems hold on tightly to patterns because they once kept us safe. This work might feel unfamiliar, tender, or even threatening to old identities. That's okay.

You're allowed to pause. You're allowed to come back. Trust the timing of your soul, not your schedule.

"I've done so much healing already. Why am I still stuck?"

Because healing isn't a checklist. It's a spiral.

You may revisit the same wound from deeper levels of awareness. You might uncover inherited patterns you didn't realize were there. That doesn't mean you're broken — it means you're going deeper. Sometimes, the final layer isn't yours. That's what this work is here to reveal.

You're not failing. You're evolving.

"Can I do this work with others? With my family?"

Yes — if they're open to it.

Some people choose to share this process with a partner, sibling, or parent. Others do it quietly, just for themselves. Both paths are valid. Just know: when you heal something in your lineage, it ripples outward. Even if no one around you joins the journey, they'll feel the shift.

Healing is personal — but its impact is collective.

"What if I start to grieve what I never had?"

That's part of the healing.

Releasing inherited beliefs sometimes reveals what you were missing — safety, validation, love without condition. That realization can be painful. But grief is proof of your capacity to feel, to care, to grow.

Let yourself mourn. Let yourself feel. Then, slowly… let yourself rebuild.

The Lineage Library: Healing Stories Passed Through Time

"The Thread in Her Veins"

The first time Ella heard the lullaby, she was three years old. Her grandmother sang it as she rocked beside the wood stove, her hands calloused, her eyes distant. The melody was soft but haunted — like it carried secrets it didn't dare speak aloud.

Years later, Ella hummed it absentmindedly while folding laundry, unaware her voice had taken on the same faraway tone. Her daughter, Lila, paused in the hallway, listening. "Where did you learn that song?" she asked.

Ella blinked. "I'm not sure," she said. "I've always known it."

But that wasn't quite true.

The song had traveled.

Through her grandmother, who sang it to soothe pain she never spoke of.
Through her mother, who hummed it while bottling up silent sacrifices.
Through Ella, who carried the ache of women who survived by staying small.

It wasn't just the song that passed down.

Ella had her grandmother's sharp cheekbones and her mother's quiet anxiety.
She flinched at loud voices the same way her mother did.
She over-apologized, overextended, over-functioned — not

because anyone asked her to, but because something in her blood whispered that love must be earned.

Each generation inherited more than eye color.

They inherited grief that was never grieved.
They inherited beliefs shaped in war, in silence, in survival.
They inherited roles: the caretaker, the peacekeeper, the one who held it all together.

One night, Lila came home in tears — overwhelmed, unsure why she felt so heavy in her young skin.

And something clicked for Ella.

She saw it — the thread. The invisible line of pain and protection weaving its way through her family tree.

That night, she didn't just hum the lullaby. She stopped.

She sat in meditation, placed a hand over her heart, and whispered:

"It ends here."

She didn't mean the song — she meant the silent contracts, the inherited wounds, the weight passed unknowingly from womb to womb.

She traced the pattern back — not in memory, but in sensation.
She felt her grandmother's sorrow, her mother's vigilance.
She cried, shook, forgave.
She returned what wasn't hers to carry.
And she chose something new.

The next morning, she taught Lila a different lullaby. One she made up on the spot. It was light, hopeful, full of joy.

Lila smiled, the sadness in her eyes softening.

And the thread?

It didn't vanish.

But it shimmered differently now — no longer a tether to pain, but a braid of wisdom, resilience, and choice.

Because one woman chose to turn inward and ask:

"What will my descendants inherit from me?"

And with that, everything changed.

"Bloodline Echoes"

It began with the dream.

Same one, over and over.
A narrow hallway. Faint candlelight.
And the sound of crying — not loud, but buried. Muffled behind the walls.

They didn't know whose it was.
Only that they always woke with the weight of it pressed against their chest.

Jade was thirty-seven.
By all accounts, life was good. A job they liked. A partner who tried. A child who laughed like bells in spring.
And yet — every morning, that same ache.

A hollowness that no amount of journaling or therapy could name.

Until the day their daughter tripped on the old rug and burst into tears. Not from pain — but from shame.

"I'm sorry, I'm sorry, I didn't mean to —"
Jade froze. The words. The panic.
Exactly like their own, as a child.

But no one ever taught her that.

It was like watching a ghost walk out of their own mouth.

That night, Jade went into the attic — a space they hadn't entered since inheriting the house. It still smelled of mothballs and time.
There, tucked in a cedar chest, were letters tied with twine.
And an old journal — their grandmother's.

They flipped through the pages.
Pages filled with apologies. Pleas to be good.
To not be a burden.
To stay small, to stay quiet.

"If I'm careful, maybe he won't get angry again."
"If I'm perfect, maybe they'll love me more."
"I must never cry in front of the children."

Jade wept.
Not just for her grandmother.
But for herself.
For her daughter.
For the women — and men — and children — and ancestors —
who had swallowed their pain for generations.

And in that attic, with the moon spilling silver through the
cracked window, Jade whispered:

"It didn't start with me.
But it can end with me."

She stood barefoot on the floorboards and breathed.
Felt the ache in her chest shift. Not vanish — but soften.
Like a knot slowly loosening.

"I release this fear.
I return this silence.
I reclaim my voice."

She lit a candle and placed it beside the journal.
She wrote a letter of her own — not of apology, but of truth.
She signed it not just with her name… but with all the names that
never had the chance.

And that night, she dreamed again.

Same hallway. Same flickering light.

But this time, the crying stopped.
And a door creaked open.
And on the other side stood a child — smiling.

Legacy isn't only what we leave behind. It's what we set free while we're still here.

"The Weight of the Axe"

He found it in the shed behind the old house:
A weathered axe, blade nicked, handle worn smooth by years of
calloused hands.

"Your grandfather used that to build the fence," his father had
said once, offhandedly, as if it were just a tool.
But Cole had always wondered — why keep it, if it was just a tool?

At 42, Cole stood in that shed, the air thick with dust and
memories, the axe still leaning in the corner like it had been
waiting for him.

He lifted it.

It was heavier than he expected.

Not just in weight — but in feeling.
Like it carried something deeper than wood and steel.
Like it remembered.

His father's silence.
His grandfather's fists.
The long lineage of men who worked hard, loved poorly, and
never said "I'm hurting."

Cole never saw his father cry.
Never heard him apologize.
He taught Cole to fix things, build things, endure things — but
not to *feel* them.

And yet, Cole remembered the way his stomach always tightened
before walking into a room with him. The way he clenched his jaw
when stressed, like his father did. The way he put work before
rest, and silence before honesty — not because he chose to, but
because something *inside him* did.

He realized it then.

The axe wasn't just passed down.

The weight was.

The belief that real men don't break.
The rule that love must be earned, not shown.
The ache of having no words for pain, so pain became identity.

Cole set the axe down.

He didn't throw it away. He wasn't angry anymore.
But he knew he wouldn't pass it on.

That night, he sat at the edge of his son's bed.
"Anything on your mind?" he asked.
His son shrugged. "Just tired."

Cole almost nodded and stood — almost kept the pattern.
But instead, he said, "Me too. I've been feeling kind of… heavy
lately. Work stuff. Life stuff. You ever feel that?"

His son blinked, surprised. Then nodded.

That was the first night they really talked.

About pressure.
About school.
About how hard it is to be strong all the time.

And the axe?
It still sits in the shed.
But now, it's just a tool.

The weight… that's been lifted.

Because one man chose not to carry the silence forward.

Because he asked himself:

"What will my son inherit from me?"

And he answered:

"Not this."

"The Envelope"

Darren had two wallets.

One was real — brown leather, worn thin, stitched by hand, the kind his father used.
The other lived in his head — invisible but heavy, full of rules he never remembered choosing.

"Money doesn't grow on trees."
"We can't afford that."
"Don't talk about money at the table."
"Save for a rainy day. But not too much. That's greedy."

His father was a saver.
But not a *builder.* Not a *dreamer.*
Just a man surviving one month to the next, always in fear of the sky falling.

Darren learned early:
Security didn't mean wealth. It meant **control**.
It meant white envelopes hidden in drawers.
Receipts folded into neat corners.
And every dollar accounted for with guilt.

So Darren rebelled.
Credit cards. Quick wins. Shiny things.
He spent to feel alive — to escape the shadow of scarcity.
But deep down, he still flinched every time the bill came.

Until the day he found his grandfather's notebook.
It was buried in a storage box after his mom passed — faded ink, columns of numbers.
But at the back of the book... a single page stood out:

"Money is not the enemy.
It's the energy we give it.

Fear taught me to hoard.
Pride taught me to pretend.
I pray Darren finds the truth we forgot."

Darren stared at the words.
His name — *written before he was even born.*
The tears came without permission.

He suddenly saw it —
Three generations of men chasing different versions of safety.
His grandfather, broken by war.
His father, bruised by recession.
Himself, strangled by debt he created trying to feel "free."

And none of them had ever actually **talked about it**.

That night, he lit a candle and placed the notebook beside his own journal.

He wrote:

"I forgive the lessons of lack.
I bless the ones who taught me.
I now choose a new story:
I am worthy of ease.
I spend with clarity.
I save with joy.
I earn in alignment.
And I give in overflow."

He closed the book.

The next morning, he made one small change.
No more ignoring the bank app.
No more guilt with groceries.
He created one envelope.
Not to hide money — but to *honor* it.

It was labeled:

"For Future Generations — with Love."

Money is never just about dollars.
It's the unspoken story we carry — and the new one we
choose to write.

"The Coat"

When Lena turned thirty-two, her mother gave her a coat.

Not just any coat — *the* coat. Long, wool, with heavy shoulders and a hem that nearly kissed the floor. "It was your grandmother's," her mother said, brushing invisible lint from the sleeve. "She wore it through the war. It's been through a lot."

Lena didn't like how it felt. The wool was coarse, itchy. The lining was torn in places. But more than that — something about it made her chest tighten when she wore it. Still, out of politeness and legacy, she draped it over her shoulders and walked out the door.

She wore it through a job she hated but didn't leave — because her father never left his.
She wore it through a breakup she didn't grieve — because her mother didn't believe in showing sadness.
She wore it through years of making herself small — because her grandmother had to be invisible to survive.

It wasn't until she saw her own daughter, one morning, trying to put on that same coat — sleeves dragging past her fingertips, shoulders swallowed whole — that Lena paused.

"What are you doing?" she asked softly.

"I want to be like you," her daughter said. "You always wear this when you're being strong."

And that's when Lena realized: strength wasn't in wearing what was handed down. It was in knowing when to take it off.

That night, Lena folded the coat and placed it in a cedar chest, along with a note:

You carried enough.
Now let the next chapter be yours to choose.

"The Love We Were Taught"

Sofia always said she didn't believe in fairy tales.
She said it with a smirk, a raised eyebrow, a glass of wine in hand.
Love, to her, was **earned** — with silence, sacrifice, and saying yes
when you wanted to scream no.

She watched her mother fade behind her father's shadow.
Watched her grandmother whisper apologies into boiling pots and
folded laundry.
Watched the women before her love like it was war —
losing a little more of themselves with every truce.

So Sofia chose differently.

She dated men who didn't stay.
She fell for ones who didn't see her.
And when someone kind came along, offering softness…
She flinched.

"Too much."
"Too soon."
"It'll never last."

One night, sitting alone on the floor with candles lit and tears that
had no clear name, she whispered aloud:

"Why does love feel like leaving myself behind?"

The room didn't answer.
But something in her body stirred — like a memory without
words.

She grabbed her journal.

Instead of writing about another breakup, she drew her mother's
hands.

Then her grandmother's.
Then her own.

All holding the same invisible thread —
love braided with duty, silence, and survival.

She wrote beneath the drawing:

"I was taught love is suffering.
I now choose love that sees, hears, and holds.
I love myself first — not as a fallback, but as a foundation."

And something shifted.

It didn't happen overnight.

But she started smiling after she spoke.
Stopped saying yes when her gut said no.
Let go of the chase.
And started listening to the small, quiet voice inside — the one
that whispered:

"You are not too much.
You are not too hard to love.
You are the one breaking the chain."

Years later, as she rocked her daughter to sleep, Sofia kissed her
forehead and whispered:

"You don't have to earn love.
You already are it."

And the thread — once tangled with pain — was rewoven with
peace.

Sometimes the greatest act of love… is remembering what love was never meant to be.
And choosing differently — for those who will come after.

"Elena always froze during conflict."

Even mild disagreement—like a tense meeting at work or a sharp tone from her partner—left her chest tight, her thoughts racing, and her voice trapped in her throat. She told herself she was "too sensitive," that she needed to toughen up.

But the reaction didn't make sense.
Her life was relatively calm. She wasn't mistreated as a child. So why did her nervous system respond as if her safety were constantly at risk?

In a moment of self-reflection, Elena tried muscle testing for the belief:

"It's dangerous to speak up."
Her body gave a strong "yes."

Then she asked:

"Is this belief mine?"
Her body said no.

When she followed the thread back—breathing, tuning in—her mind flashed an image: her grandmother, a quiet woman from Eastern Europe who had survived war, loss, and decades of swallowing words to avoid conflict. A woman who had taught her daughter (Elena's mother) that silence kept you safe. That it was better to endure than to resist.

And suddenly, it made sense.
The fear in her voice wasn't hers. It was inherited.

Elena used the AuricIons Release method, step-by-step.
She grounded herself. She thanked the women who came before her. She whispered to the old belief, "You kept them safe, but I

don't need you anymore."
And when she spoke her new truth—"It's safe to be seen. My voice matters"—something softened.

Over time, she noticed subtle changes:
She held eye contact longer.
She said no when she meant it.
Her partner even said, "You seem more… you."

That belief didn't vanish overnight.
But for the first time, it wasn't in charge.

"The Body Remembers"

No one in Mateo's family talked about pain.

His grandfather lost a leg in the war and never mentioned it.
His father worked through migraines, back spasms, and ulcers
with a tight jaw and a bottle of antacids in the truck.

And Mateo?

He ignored the chest tightness.
Laughed off the tension headaches.
Called his panic attacks "just being tired."

He wore strength like a badge —
until his body issued a quiet rebellion.

It began small: tightness in his gut, then a racing heart, then a
collapse in the grocery store aisle.
The doctor said it was stress.
Mateo said it was nothing.

But one night, after the third time he couldn't catch his breath
lying in bed, he asked the air:

"What am I holding that's not mine?"

He remembered his father, sitting silently at the kitchen table after
his brother died.
He remembered his mother, swallowing her sadness and saying,
"We just have to keep going."
He remembered the phrase he'd grown up hearing:

"We're not the kind of people who fall apart."

And it hit him —
He'd inherited their silence.

Not just their eyes or blood type,
but their blueprint for how to **ignore pain** until it broke you.

The next day, Mateo did something no man in his family ever had:
He booked a therapy session.

He also bought a journal — not because he liked writing, but
because he needed to *speak* to someone, even if it was the page.

He learned about the nervous system.
Learned that fight-or-flight can be passed on like eye color.
That a body raised in stress learns to live in survival.

And slowly, with breathwork, with tears, with truth, Mateo began
to soften.

He walked more.
Laughed louder.
Rested without guilt.

And when his nephew came over one weekend, tripped, and
started crying —
Mateo didn't say, "You're fine."
He knelt, held him, and said:

"It's okay to hurt. It's okay to feel."

Something shifted in that moment.
Not just in the boy —
but in the bloodline.

Because sometimes healing doesn't look like green juice or
gym sessions.
Sometimes healing is just learning to listen when your body
whispers —
and answering with kindness instead of silence.

"The Quiet Knock"

Michael had never raised his voice.

Not as a boy, not as a man. Not even when his first love walked out the door, or when his father lay in the hospital bed with tubes where words used to be. He was the calm one. The solid one. The dependable one.

People admired that about him. He wore stillness like armor. But inside, it was different. Inside, there was a quiet knock he'd been ignoring for years.

It came in the form of tight shoulders.
Of never knowing what he really wanted.
Of a feeling that he had to hold it all together—or else.

One afternoon, while helping his aunt clean out the family attic, Michael found an old journal—his grandfather's. He barely knew the man. A stern face in black-and-white photos, always looking slightly away from the camera.

He flipped through brittle pages until one line stopped him cold:

"I was taught that men must be pillars. Even if the weight breaks them."

Michael sat there, holding the sentence like a mirror. For the first time, he saw it: the invisible hand on his shoulder, guiding him toward silence, sacrifice, suppression.

It wasn't his hand. It never had been.

And slowly, he began to move differently.

He started saying "I don't know."
He told a friend when he was struggling.

He stood in the mirror and let himself cry—for the first time in years.

That quiet knock? It wasn't weakness. It was his soul trying to be heard through the noise of generations.

And finally, he opened the door.

Practice Prompts + Journal Integration

Let your body speak. Let your truth emerge.

Now that you've learned how to use muscle testing to discern the origin of a belief, it's time to integrate the process with self-reflection. These prompts aren't just mental exercises — they're invitations to **connect with your body's wisdom**, your lineage's influence, and your soul's truth.

Use these after testing a belief. Write freely, without judgment. Let whatever surfaces come through.

✦ Prompt 1: What belief or emotion did I test?
Describe what came up for you. Use specific wording (e.g., "I believe I have to fix everything," or "I feel unsafe when I speak up.")

✦ Prompt 2: What was the result of the muscle test?
Did your body say it was self-created or inherited? How did that feel to discover?

✦ Prompt 3: If this belief didn't begin with me, whose might it be?
Allow your intuition to answer. Think about the tone, the behavior, or the story that matches this belief. Does it feel like mom's? Dad's? An ancestral echo?

✦ Prompt 4: What purpose has this belief served — and is it still serving me?
Sometimes, we carry beliefs for protection, connection, or survival. Acknowledge that role… then decide if it's time to release it.

✦ Prompt 5: What would my life feel like without this belief?
Visualize your life — your body, your relationships, your energy — without this inherited pattern. Who would you be if you didn't carry this?

✦ Prompt 6: What do I choose to believe now?
Write a new belief. One that comes from truth, not trauma. One that feels like yours.

✦ Prompt 7: What do I choose to believe now?
Write your new truth — not as wishful thinking, but as an embodied declaration. One that resonates with your energy, not your fear. One that feels like *you*.

✦ Prompt 8: What action can I take to embody this new belief?
It could be a boundary, a ritual, a conversation, or simply noticing the shift in your body. Healing becomes real when it reaches the physical plane.

✦ Prompt 9: What energy or emotion do I consistently feel that doesn't seem to match my life experience?
Identify patterns of sadness, fear, anger, or shame that seem to appear without a clear cause. Is it possible you've inherited them?

✦ Prompt 10: What family belief have I silently agreed to, even if it doesn't align with my truth?
"I must always put others first." "We don't talk about emotions." "Success requires sacrifice."
Explore where you might be living someone else's rulebook.

✦ Prompt 11: Whose love or approval have I felt I had to earn — and at what cost?
Go deeper into any patterns of people-pleasing, perfectionism, or self-sacrifice. Whose story are you still trying to fulfill?

✦ **Prompt 12: What unspoken family or cultural rules shaped who I thought I had to be?**
Think beyond words — to what was modeled, implied, or expected. What would it mean to challenge or rewrite those rules?

✦ **Prompt 13: What physical sensations do I experience when I focus on this belief or memory?**
Tight chest? Nausea? Pressure in your back? Let the body speak. Every sensation is a messenger.

✦ **Prompt 14: What's the first memory I have that matches this belief or emotional experience?**
Even if it's fuzzy or symbolic — write it down. There may be a thread to follow.

✦ **Prompt 15: What generational pattern am I being called to break?**
This isn't about blame — it's about legacy. What ends with you?

✦ **Prompt 16: If I could send one message of healing to my ancestors, what would it be?**
Let your heart speak. This can be part of your release.

✦ **Prompt 17: What qualities or strengths have I inherited that I want to carry forward?**
Not everything passed down is a wound. Name the wisdom, gifts, or resilience you're proud to claim.

✦ **Prompt 18: What part of me is asking to be witnessed right now?**
Is it the *inner child* who never felt safe?
The *protector* who learned to stay quiet to keep the peace?
The *healer* who tries to fix everyone else while carrying silent pain?
The *truth-teller* who's been waiting years to finally speak?

These are all parts of you — sacred, wise, and deserving of voice. Let your pen become their microphone. Write as though you're giving that part of you a stage.
What would they say if they finally felt safe enough to be heard?

You might be surprised by what rises when you pause and truly ask:
Who inside me needs the floor today?

There's no wrong answer. Just truth, waiting to be known.

✦ **Prompt 19: What memory surfaces when I tune into this belief or emotion?**
It might be a full scene or just a flicker — a scent, a look, a phrase that echoes in your body.
Don't overanalyze. Just describe it.
Does it feel like yours… or someone else's?
How old do you feel in that moment?
Let the memory guide you toward what's asking to be released.

✦ **Prompt 20: What does my body do when I think about this belief?**
Do your shoulders tense?
Does your jaw clench?
Does your chest tighten or your breath get shallow?
Let your body be your guide — it often remembers what the mind forgets.
Describe the sensations, and ask what they might be trying to tell you.

✦ **Prompt 21: What energetic weight am I ready to set down?**
Is it guilt that isn't yours?
A responsibility you never chose?
A silence you inherited or learned to keep?
Name it.
Then write, *"I release this now, with love."*
See what shifts inside you.

Resource Guide

Support for Your Healing Journey

Whether you're just beginning or deepening your practice, the following resources are here to support your path forward. Healing is never meant to be walked alone.

Recommended Reading

Books that echo and expand the themes of emotional inheritance, generational healing, and body-based wisdom:

- **It Didn't Start With You** by Mark Wolynn
- **The Body Keeps the Score** by Bessel van der Kolk
- **My Grandmother's Hands** by Resmaa Menakem
- **Eastern Body, Western Mind** by Anodea Judith
- **The Biology of Belief** by Dr. Bruce Lipton
- **Radical Compassion** by Tara Brach
- **When the Body Says No** by Dr. Gabor Maté
- **Energy Medicine** by Donna Eden
- **Waking the Tiger: Healing Trauma** by Peter Levine
- **Ancestral Medicine** by Daniel Foor

Websites + Practitioners

- constancesantego.ca – Tools, courses, and intuitive healing support with Dr. Constance Santego
- emdria.org – Find certified EMDR trauma therapists
- anewdawntherapy.ca – Somatic and generational healing resources
- muscletesting101.com – Beginner's guide to self-testing

Terms

Here is a clear and grounded explanation of terms, especially as they relate to ancestral healing, energetic work, and quantum medicine:

Cultural Trauma / Collective Imprint

Trauma not just passed down through family, but carried by entire groups due to shared histories (e.g., colonization, displacement, racism, genocide). Often sits in the collective field, affecting descendants on physical and energetic levels.

Energetic Block

A disruption or stagnation in the flow of life force (chi, prana, etc.) due to unresolved emotions, traumas, or inherited fears. It can show up as resistance, pain, or a "stuck" feeling.

Energetic Imprint

The lasting signature of an experience, belief, or emotion embedded in the energy field. Unlike residue, an imprint is often more structural and can shape behaviors or life patterns until consciously released.

Energy Residue

Energy residue is the lingering energetic imprint left behind from an experience—yours or someone else's—that wasn't fully processed or cleared. It's like emotional "dust" in your system that affects how you feel or respond in the present.

Example: Still feeling uneasy or anxious in situations that remind you of past trauma, even if logically you know you're safe.

Emotional Scars

These are the emotional imprints left behind by pain, betrayal, grief, fear, or rejection. While some scars fade with time and healing, others remain as unconscious influences on how you relate to yourself and the world.

Example: Avoiding love because of past heartbreak or rejection, even if you deeply want connection.

Energetic Weight

Energetic weight refers to the heaviness or burden carried in your energetic field due to unresolved trauma, beliefs, or experiences. It affects your vitality, joy, clarity, and even your physical health.

Example: Feeling exhausted or stuck without an obvious physical reason—because your system is overloaded with inherited or unprocessed energy.

Genetic Memory

This refers to the idea that memories, responses, and emotional patterns can be biologically encoded and passed through DNA. It supports the theory that you can *feel or act* based on ancestral experiences you never personally lived through.

Example: Feeling panic around authority figures with no obvious reason, but your lineage includes persecution or oppression.

Inheritance

Inheritance refers to the passing down of not only genetic traits but also emotional beliefs, coping mechanisms, and energetic imprints through your family lineage. It's what you may have *absorbed*, not chosen—from your parents, grandparents, or cultural community.

Example: Being taught to avoid conflict, hide emotions, or overwork, even if it's never been openly spoken.

Intergenerational Trauma

This is trauma that is passed down from one generation to another, often through behavior, nervous system regulation, or silence. It doesn't have to be verbally communicated to be inherited—it can be *felt*, *modeled*, or *stored* in the body's energy field.

Example: A grandparent's experience of war or poverty creating a survival mentality that shapes family dynamics generations later.

Internalized Voice

A voice you've taken on as your own—often from a caregiver, authority figure, or cultural norm. It becomes the inner critic or voice of limitation, even when the original source is no longer present.

Karmic Loop

A recurring life situation, lesson, or relationship dynamic that reflects unresolved karmic energy. These loops tend to repeat until awareness, action, or forgiveness transforms them.

Memory Fields: Physical, Emotional, Spiritual, and Mental

Each part of your being holds memory:

- **Physical Memory** – Stored in muscles, posture, chronic pain, or illness.
- **Emotional Memory** – Felt through mood swings, overreactions, or emotional numbness.
- **Spiritual Memory** – Held in your soul's journey and energetic imprint; includes past lives, karmic contracts, and intuition.
- **Mental Memory** – Reflected in your thoughts, belief systems, and internal narratives.

These memories are layered and can be activated by current events, sensations, or even words.

Pattern

A *pattern* is a recurring behavior, thought, or emotional response that shows up across time or situations—often without conscious awareness. Patterns may originate in your own life or be inherited from others. They act like subconscious programs running in the background.

Example: Always people-pleasing, fearing abandonment, or self-sabotaging before success.

Protective Mechanism

An unconscious emotional or energetic strategy developed to survive or prevent pain. Often adaptive at the time, but becomes limiting when carried forward unnecessarily.

Psycho-Spiritual Patterning

The intertwining of psychological experiences and spiritual themes—how emotional trauma intersects with spiritual lessons, identity, or awakening.

Somatic Memory

The body's way of remembering trauma or emotional events. Somatic memories are often triggered by sensations, smells, or touch, and can lead to automatic body reactions even when the mind has no conscious recall.

Spiritual Echoes

These are subtle, recurring impressions that may originate from past lives, karmic lessons, or soul-level agreements. They often show up as intuitive knowings, irrational fears, or recurring themes in your spiritual path.

Example: Feeling drawn to a specific place or person with no known connection—or being triggered by something you've never experienced directly.

Soul Contract

An agreement made on a soul level (consciously or unconsciously) before birth or during key life transitions, meant to help you evolve or learn something specific. These may show up in relationships, roles, or repeated life themes.

Subconscious Programming

These are deeply embedded mental and emotional scripts that influence your thoughts, actions, and emotions—often inherited or conditioned during early childhood, and not accessible through ordinary awareness.

◆ MESSAGE FROM THE AUTHOR

If you've made it this far, thank you. Truly.

Writing this book was not just an act of sharing what I've learned—it was a deep remembering of my own. Each section reflects not only the journeys of the many clients and students I've had the honour of working with, but also my own path through the tangled web of inherited beliefs, buried emotions, and soul-level truths.

I wrote *More Than Bloodlines* for the person who has done the work—and still feels something lingering. For the person who can't explain the ache but knows it's real. For the one who's begun to wonder, *"What if this pain isn't mine?"*

This book is an invitation to look beneath the surface of your story and listen to the quiet wisdom of your body and your soul. It's not about fixing yourself—it's about meeting yourself, fully and compassionately, with the understanding that what you carry might not have started with you… but you get to choose how it ends.

You are not broken. You are becoming.

Thank you for walking this path with me.

In healing,
Dr. Constance Santego

About The Author

Dr. Constance Santego is a renowned natural medicine doctor, spiritual teacher, and energy healing expert with over three decades of experience helping clients and students uncover the hidden roots of emotional and energetic pain. She is the creator of the **AuricIons Release** method—a 9-step process that blends quantum medicine, muscle testing, vibrational healing, and deep subconscious work to transform inherited patterns at their root.

A lifelong researcher of generational trauma, ancestral memory, and soul evolution, Dr. Santego's teachings bridge ancient wisdom with modern healing techniques. Through her bestselling books, transformative courses, and international workshops, she has guided thousands to remember who they were before the world told them otherwise.

In *More Than Bloodlines*, Dr. Santego offers a powerful guide for those carrying emotional burdens that don't quite feel like their own. Drawing from real-world client experiences, spiritual insight, and her signature healing process, she invites readers to break free from the stories they didn't choose—and reclaim the truth of who they are.

She is also the founder of Maximillian Enterprises, a platform for conscious authors and educators, and continues to lead a legacy of awakening through her writing, teaching, and visionary healing work.

She currently resides in Kelowna, B.C., where she continues to write, teach, mentor, and inspire others to share their stories—and their truth—with the world.

Website: www.constancesantego.ca
YouTube: @ConstanceSantego

"The River I Chose to Cross"

There once was a woman who stood at the edge of a river.

Behind her was a land where the ground was cracked with old pain — stories buried but not forgotten, wounds passed from hand to hand like heirlooms. The sky was heavy there. Smiles were tight. Love was often quiet, and fear ran deep beneath the surface.

This was the land of her ancestors. A place where silence was survival, where duty was louder than dreams, and where pain was inherited like eye color or height.

She carried it all. Not because she wanted to, but because no one had ever told her she didn't have to.

Until one day, she looked into the eyes of her children. Then, her grandchildren.

And she knew: **it ends with me.**

So she turned toward the river — the one so few dared to cross. The one made of grief and growth, memories and unlearning. Its waters were cold and unfamiliar. But she stepped in anyway.

She went to counseling. She read the books. She took the courses. She sat with her younger self and whispered, *"You didn't deserve the pain. But you do deserve peace."*

And slowly, slowly, she crossed that river.

She left behind the belief that she wasn't enough.
She laid down the idea that love had to hurt.
She set free the need to carry everyone else's weight.

When she reached the other side, her hands were empty—but her heart was full. And she turned around and built a bridge.

Not a perfect one, but strong enough.

And someday, when her children and grandchildren walk their own paths and find themselves near the same river, they'll see that bridge. They'll know someone came before them—not to carry their pain, but to clear the way.

And if they ask how it was built, she'll smile and say:

"With truth. With courage. And with love so deep, it refused to let the past shape your future."

ALSO AVAILABLE

AuricIons

Unlocking Subconscious Healing Through Quantum Medicine

Trade Paperback ISBN: 978-1-990062-49-0
eBook ISBN 978-1-990062-50-6

Play the game *Ikona* – Discover Your Inner Genie

For additional information on

Constance Santego's

wide range of Motivational Products, Coaching Sessions, Spiritual Retreats,
Live Events and Educational Programs

Go to

www.ConstanceSantego.ca

Follow on Instagram - Constance_Santego and
Facebook - constancesantegoo

Subscribe and receive Free Information and Meditations on my
YouTube Channel - Constance Santego